alongside

"*Alongside* is equal parts practicality, encouragement, and challenge—and desperately needed! All I can say is I wish I'd had it earlier, I will refer to it often, and I will share it every chance I get."

–**Keith Ferrin**
Author, Speaker, Storyteller
www.keithferrin.com
Seattle, WA

"As I grow older, the need to come alongside suffering friends has increased in frequency. *Alongside* provides rock solid, practical advice that will give you confidence as you seek to genuinely love people as they walk through the dark valleys of life. I will keep this book as a handy resource for knowing how to love people when they need it most."

–**Ken Davis**
Speaker, Award-winning Author
Trainer in the art and business of public speaking
Nashville, TN

"In *Alongside*, Sarah Beckman finds a way to put joy and grace into a painful topic. Reading it is like sitting down to a cup of coffee with a friend and going deep to share personal stories and very practical advice. This book is so helpful because of the RANGE of information it covers. Sarah creates a beautiful balance of personal stories and real life experience which allows everyone to find someone to identify with."

–**Rita Ward**
Nurse, Former Licensed Psychologist
Eden Prairie, MN

"Sarah has been using people's lives as the canvas on which to help create a new reality for them for over a decade—now you can read about it."

–**Eric Samuel Timm**
Author, Orator, Artist
Rochester, MN

"*Alongside* is a beautiful work of art that touches our souls while guiding our hearts, hands, and words to come alongside those who are hurting and grieving. Sarah gently and expertly answers the questions we wrestle with regarding 'how to' genuinely care for those in pain—beyond casseroles, cards and platitudes. Walking with others in their most difficult moments requires courage to wade in while feeling ill-equipped, and grace to continue on in moments of uncertainty. *Alongside* offers wisdom I wish I'd known years ago and insights and practical tips for making this journey with others."

–**Susie Miller, MA, MDiv**
Author, Coach, Speaker
www.susiemiller.com
Washington, DC

"It seems that in my circle of friends, as soon as one person is coming out of crisis, it's just that time where someone else is going in. Having several friends who have gone through overwhelming circumstances in the past couple of years, I know what a valuable resource this book will be. *Alongside* is designed with you in mind—the friend who wants to be there for their friend, but doesn't always know the next best step. Have this book on hand for the next time someone you love is in the midst of a crisis. You will go from feeling helpless to hopeful."

–**Kathi Lipp**
Speaker and Author of *Clutter Free* and *The Husband Project*
San Jose, CA

"For anyone who finds themselves tugged by the challenges and opportunities to help others, this book is a wonderful resource. It is both inspiring and practical. In these pages you will find comfort and checklists for connecting with those in need. Sarah writes with candid compassion from years of experience and a heart held by the love of Jesus.

–**Joel Quie**
Pastor of Prairie Lutheran Church
Eden Prairie, MN

"*Alongside* is a must-read resource for those of us who have a suffering friend or family member. Brimming with practical insights and advice from real people who have experienced tragedy, this indispensible guide helps us compassionately navigate stormy waters with our loved ones in crisis.

–Kerri Kustra, MD
Albuquerque, NM

"*Alongside* is a wonderful book full of resources to help you help others. Consider this: great cooks check their recipes, sea captains review their charts, and air pilots run through their checklist on every flight. Similarly, *Alongside* equips and enables you to navigate with words and actions a more intentional and beneficial response as you love your 'neighbor'—no matter the trial."

–David Pierce
John Maxwell Team Certified Coach, Speaker, Teacher
Ordained Minister, Sales Executive
San Antonio, TX

"Many of us can be hesitant helpers, not because we don't care, but because we don't know how to help in time of crisis. Sarah's book is full of practical and sensitive tools for reaching out to others in need. It also offers invaluable advice on how to avoid doing the wrong things with the best of intentions. If you want to be more intentional about loving people the way Jesus calls us to love, read *Alongside*! Then keep it handy for future reference. You'll want to go back to it again and again."

–Karen Warin
Ministry Director, The Navigators
Faith@Work for Women in the Workplace
Albuquerque, NM

"As a pastor in full-time ministry for 20 years, I unfortunately learned how to come alongside others by trial and (quite a bit of) error! How

I wish I had this book 20 years ago! Now serving as a lay-leader in our church, I am excited about this resource to help equip those parts of the Body of Christ who may not be naturally inclined in the areas of compassion and caretaking. As a communication coach and consultant I am impressed by the research and practical benefit of this book.

–Brent McCall, Ph.D
President of Presentation Impact
Sandia Park, NM

"*Wanting* to care, but *not knowing how to care* is a conundrum that often prevents us from not following through with our best intentions when our friends or loved ones are facing trial. This book will be a helpful resource for those who feel a *nudge* to do *something*, but can't quite figure out the timing, appropriateness or specifics for putting this *nudge* into action. In *Alongside,* you'll be captivated by Sarah's personal journey on both sides of the fence. You'll find compelling reasons you should care for your neighbor and also a wealth of practical ways to do so. As a pastor, I know this book will be an invaluable resource for individuals and serving teams as they plan care for friends, neighbors, the community and each other."

–Linnea Grey, MS
Associate Pastor of Northgate Church
Ramsey, MN

"*Alongside* is both inspiring and practical. Each chapter is full of great ideas, examples, and easy to follow guidelines for how to show love to our neighbors. It will motivate you to be intentional about being the hands and feet of Jesus to people you meet everyday who are facing trial."

–Vince Carrillo
Campus Pastor of Sagebrush Community Church
Albuquerque, NM

"*Alongside* will be your new go-to staple on the nightstand! Sarah has walked the walk, and from her experience, she has created an accessible guide for men, women, young, and seasoned that's both engaging to read and filled to the brim with practical suggestions, talking points, warnings, and real-life examples you'll relate to. You will turn to this helpful guide again and again as those around you navigate the rough waters of life."

–**Mallory Polk**
Creative and Organized Mother of Four
Instagram: @ thisamericanwife
St Louis, MO

"In a world where we are so connected to technology that we have lost touch with real relationships, I love that Sarah is tackling a simple truth! Coming alongside people going through various trials should come naturally for those of us who love Jesus. Yet if you are like me, it can be very intimidating and difficult to step outside my comfort zone and walk alongside others. *Alongside* encourages and challenges us to fulfill the Great Commandment as we walk this journey called life. Sarah's practical instruction makes this a must-read!"

–**Laura Laffoon**
Speaker, Author, Co-founder of Celebrate Ministries
Alma, MI

"Life isn't a one-person job. As a parent and friend, I've learned the most valuable way to help people going through trials is to be present. But how? Sarah Beckman's *Alongside* provides valuable insight and practical approaches to caring for those who need it most."

–**Michael Hyatt**
Co-author of USA Today Bestseller, *Living Forward*

alongside

A Practical Guide for
Loving Your Neighbor in their Time of Trial

sarah beckman

New York

alongside
A Practical Guide for Loving Your Neighbor in their Time of Trial

Published in New York, New York, by Morgan James Publishing. Morgan James and The Entrepreneurial Publisher are trademarks of Morgan James, LLC.
www.MorganJamesPublishing.com

The Morgan James Speakers Group can bring authors to your live event. For more information or to book an event visit The Morgan James Speakers Group at www.TheMorganJamesSpeakersGroup.com.

Shelfie

A **free** eBook edition is available
with the purchase of this print book.

CLEARLY PRINT YOUR NAME ABOVE IN UPPER CASE

Instructions to claim your free eBook edition:
1. Download the Shelfie app for Android or iOS
2. Write your name in **UPPER CASE** above
3. Use the Shelfie app to submit a photo
4. Download your eBook to any device

ISBN 978-1-63047-983-1 paperback
ISBN 978-1-63047-984-8 eBook
ISBN 978-1-63047-985-5 hardcover
Library of Congress Control Number:
2016902782

Cover Design by:
Chris Treccani
www.3dogdesign.net

Interior Design by:
Bonnie Bushman
The Whole Caboodle Graphic Design

In an effort to support local communities, raise awareness and funds, Morgan James Publishing donates a percentage of all book sales for the life of each book to Habitat for Humanity Peninsula and Greater Williamsburg.

Get involved today! Visit
www.MorganJamesBuilds.com

For Craig—my Barney.
Without your encouragement,
this book would never have come to be.

contents

foreword

When I first met Kate, she was already knee deep in crisis.

She showed up in the Tuesday night Bible study I led, Bible in hand and scarf on her head. She'd recently moved with her husband from out of state and was anxious to find a circle of new friends. I felt a near instant kinship at our meeting, her sweet spirit and sincere faith drawing me to her like a moth to a light. After hearing her story—a story thick with the diagnosis and grim prognosis of "pancreatic cancer"—I determined to find ways to help.

Problem was I didn't know what to do. I knew how to lead a Bible study, but how do you help a woman with cancer? What do you say to someone who might not live? You pray, of course. You always pray. But I wanted to do more, something tangible to ease her suffering. But the only thing I could think to do was to cook. It's the one thing I do when I don't know what to do. So when Kate mentioned in passing that she craved bread during her constant cancer treatments, I set out to make the best bread she'd ever had. Pancreatic cancer is brutal to the body, the digestive system in particular. But homemade bread? She couldn't get enough of it.

So I made loaves and loaves of it, along with not a few dozen homemade chocolate chip cookies. And I delivered both to her house (to her husband's delight) as often as I could. It seemed like such a small thing, an insignificant offering for a woman fighting for her life. Surely there was more to be done, but what? I didn't know and was too afraid to ask. So I kept making bread and cookies with gusto, hoping it somehow helped.

Little did I know her battle would end up a lengthy one. Not two years or five. But thirteen, and *counting.*

And little did I know my own battles were soon to come.

Eight years and countless bread offerings into my friend's cancer journey, I began my own. With a single unexpected phone call from a doctor two days before Thanksgiving, my life turned upside down. One moment I was an ordinary thirty-nine year old mom and wife. The next I was a cancer victim fighting for my life.

It's one thing to observe a crisis, another to experience one. Just that fast, I turned from self-sufficient bread-maker to helpless patient. Immediately I resented it. It was much easier to make bread for others than to be in a position to ask for it myself. But the battle I was to fight would be long and grueling. And before all was said and done, I needed more help than I ever imagined.

Rather than pancreatic cancer, mine was cancer of the tongue. And in the span of five years, it came back three separate times. Each occurrence proved worse that the one before, each requiring more extensive surgery and treatment, each demanding a grueling recovery that, at the end, would leave me a different woman than I'd been before. By the time all was said and done, I'd lost two-thirds of my tongue, my ability to speak, swallow and eat normally, as well as approximately 80% of my taste. In addition, I had multiple incisions on my neck to remove lymph nodes, incisions and skin grafts on my left arm and thigh, nerve damage in my arm and neck, not to mention a feeding tube for five months and a tracheostomy opening for nearly two.

Almost overnight, our ordinary, suburban family was turned upside down. Physically, it would take me more than a full year to recover from surgeries, hospital stays, radiation, and chemotherapy treatments. Even when I began to reenter life again, I knew I'd never physically be the same. Emotionally, the road of recovery would take far longer. And I suspected my heart and mind would never fully move past the trauma of all it'd endured.

My time as a patient, although riddled with losses, also brought tremendous gains. I learned what it feels like to be on the receiving end of comfort, to boldly ask for help, and then to graciously receive it. In the course of our years of near-constant crisis, countless family members, neighbors, and friends came to our family's aid. We wouldn't have survived without such beautiful displays of burden-sharing. Whether it was the friend who flew hundreds of miles to sit with me in silence during my recovery, the hundreds of cards and letters received in the mail, or the neighbors who took care of meals and laundry, each offering of help and presence—regardless of how big or small—eased our suffering a bit.

But in the midst of these stunning examples of support, there were many others that fell flat. Although well-intentioned, these haphazard offerings carried more sting than relief. Like the woman who repeatedly tried to convince me, both privately and publicly, that my chosen treatment plan was wrong. Or the friend who desperately wanted me to celebrate the fact that I was alive rather than crying for all that had been lost. Or the countless friends and strangers who felt it their duty to let me know what food to eat and oils to apply to cure my own disease, the implication being that I'd done something to cause it in the first place.

Their heart was right, their approach wrong. However, I wasn't angry. Yes, it hurt, but I knew from my friendship with Kate how utterly overwhelming it is to attempt to meet the gaping needs of someone in crisis. You want so badly to bring relief, but you haven't a clue how to do so. Worse, you're terrified of getting it wrong and, somehow, adding to their pain. Thus, I also learned how to extend grace to the givers, both to myself and so many others.

But perhaps the greatest lesson I gained is this one: If you and I would dare to engage in a conversation, to ask questions and listen to the answers, we could do better. We could learn what it looks like to serve and love one another well, even in great pain. We could learn how to walk alongside, both in heart and in practical support. We could learn how to identify our own needs in crisis and then communicate them well. And we could all learn how to embrace a measure of personal discomfort in order to ease the discomfort of another.

Enter *Alongside*.

With love for both the person in pain and the people who care for them, my friend Sarah Beckman has crafted a heartfelt and practical book to help bridge the gap between good intentions and beautiful relationship. Not only does she have a wealth of personal experience, she's also invested in countless in-depth interviews. In short, she's done the work so you and I don't have to. As a result, *Alongside* is a hard-won collection of wisdom for those who want to turn the isolation of crisis into an opportunity for life-giving connection.

Don't miss the significance and the potential of what you hold. Read it, highlighter in hand. Take notes. Put it into practice. Then, come back and read it again. You won't always get it right, I'll guarantee you that. But in trying and learning and growing, you'll honor someone's suffering and, perhaps, prepare yourself for your own.

Like homemade bread hot from the oven, you'll satisfy the suffering soul's craving for the presence of another. In the process, I think you'll find a little soul-satisfaction for yourself as well.

With you,
Michele Cushatt
March 25, 2016
Author of *Undone: A Story of Making Peace With An Unexpected Life*
(Zondervan, 2015)

introduction

I'm writing a book, and I need your help.

I remember the moment with crystal clarity. Sitting at my kitchen counter in my New Mexico home, laptop open, fingers racing over keyboard, I typed an email to a group of trusted friends who'd faced plenty of hardship and might be willing to talk about it.

I also knew a thing or two about what it looked like to be in need as well as to help others going through hard times. I lived through 11 bedridden weeks before the birth of my third child, then four back surgeries, all within a span of six years. I walked the cancer journey up close and personal with three dear friends and family members in as many years. And I'd had the holy privilege of being intimately involved in the last months, days, and hours of several peoples' lives. Now it was time to share what I had learned with anyone who'd read it.

I'm writing a book, and I need your help. Will you tell me exactly what was helpful and not-so-helpful to you during your most difficult life experience?

The first email response came within an hour.

Over the next days, months, and years, my friends stepped up. Big time. I interviewed folks on the phone, in person, via email, over coffee, lunch, at the park, by the pool, via Skype, and on Facebook. They talked, I listened. I asked, they answered. They cried, I cried.

As I began to consolidate and categorize their quips, quotes, suggestions, and experiences, the harmony of their common story—regardless of circumstance—began to emerge.

The research didn't stop, hasn't stopped, even as I write. Because life moves on, and, sadly, people I know and love continue to face hardship each and every day. But one thing is for certain. Their story, my story, needs to be told.

Alongside is not a magic formula to make everything better. It is helpful suggestions born out of life-changing experiences. Personal testimonies wrought from time in the trenches, either helping or being helped. Valuable insights shared from humble places.

I am indebted to the beautiful, brave souls willing to share their journeys to make this book possible. Because of their courage and insight, you have in your hands the tools you need to help the ones you love when they need it most. It is my prayer that you will see your loved one's times of trial as a new opportunity for you to love and serve—not as a crisis of personal ability.

But be prepared. Helping others will change you and how you view your "neighbor" in times to come. As you step out in faith, God will shine through your actions, words, and deeds as you become the literal hands and feet of Christ.

God bless you in your journey. I'm honored to come alongside and walk with you.

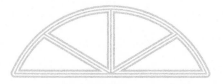

Part 1

first things first

Trust in the LORD with all your heart, and do not
lean on your own understanding. In all your ways
acknowledge him, and he will make straight your paths.
–Proverbs 3:5–6 ESV

Chapter 1

the heart of the matter

We love because He first loved us.
−1 John 4:19 HCSB

didn't realize I was lost until God found me.

I grew up in the church and believed in God. I even prayed to Him when I needed help. But as an adult, I succumbed to a lukewarm faith—focused on convenience more than substance, obligation more than conviction, me more than God.

Discovering a deeper faith happened slowly at first, as we faced trials and others began to love us through them. Then, as we began to attend church more regularly and make Sunday more of a priority, we started to hear what the pastor was saying, not just to other people, but *to us*. One day, like a dam breaking forth, I was overcome by my need to be taken up into this powerful force—all in for God. I was done living halfway. I swore my life would never be the same.

That was 14 years ago.

In the Bible, James talks about an outpouring of actions as a result of life-saving faith. That was the way it happened for me. I wanted everyone to know about the Man I had recently met and how He saved me. I was like a girl with a brand new engagement ring, wanting to show everyone the reason for my happiness. In my case though, it wasn't a ring but a guy named Jesus.

I used to think people who used His name were "Jesus Freaks," like the 90's song by Christian band DC Talk. But once He had a true hold on me, I didn't care anymore. I wasn't going back to the old way of doing things, depending only on myself and miserably trying to control all my circumstances. (Which never worked, by the way.) I was done with that life.

I began reading and studying the Bible for the very first time, and I was amazed by all the practical information I found in it. I did have my share of questions though. There were some phrases that deeply perplexed me. I thought I'd never be able to discover how to live them out.

Commanded to Love

One conversation Jesus had with some of the religious leaders of his day seemed to be quite important:

> 'Teacher, which is the most important commandment in the Law of Moses?' Jesus replied, 'You must love the Lord your God with all your heart, all your soul, and all your mind. This is the first and greatest commandment. A second is equally important: Love your neighbor as yourself. The entire law

and all the demands of the prophets are based on these two commandments.' (Matthew 22:36-40 NLT)

When reading that passage, I had several thoughts. First, Jesus said loving your neighbor was second in importance only to loving God. Second, He didn't say exactly *how* we were to love our neighbor. And finally, loving my neighbor seemed pretty hard to do.

I'm an all or nothing kinda girl. This has caused me trouble at times, but Jesus' simple directive to "love my neighbor as myself" fueled an especially deep need in me. I wanted to put meat on its bones—to understand its full meaning.

My quest didn't deliver black and white answers, but over time, I began to see that love was the essential ingredient. And it could be expressed in many different forms. Alarmingly, I have also discovered many who merely give lip service to this seemingly simple command. Yes, we all know we ought to love our neighbor, but if we are brave enough to admit it, we don't actually understand *how*. And if we do figure out what to do, we fear we might actually *have to do it.*

Loving your neighbor is a task that can be daunting, confusing, scary, and vulnerable. And it's a whole lot easier to read it, know it, and talk about it than do it.

But I don't want to be caught making excuses for why I'm not doing what God said. After all, He's very clear: love Me and love others. Wholly living out our faith hinges on these two commands. That's why I believe reaching out to help others is more than just "doing the right thing." It is our God-given responsibility. And in a hurting and broken world, it's essential.

Reaching out to help others is more than just "doing the right thing." It is our God-given responsibility.

When Faith Isn't Your Motivation

If you've opened this book and are surprised by all this talk of Jesus, you may not become convinced of the necessity of loving your neighbor because He commanded it. Maybe you're caring for a friend in need simply because you love them and you know it's the right thing to do. If you've put God on the back burner in your life or have placed your faith in something else—career, friends, spouse, image, or even your own abilities—I want to tell you this: God is using you whether you know it or not. He instilled that penchant for good. He created that heart for others. He made you a philanthropic-minded being.

I pray for the time in your life where you recognize His power at work through you and perhaps even His power displayed in your own weakness. Your Maker will never stop seeking you. He desires to know you and be known by you.

But no matter where you stand in your spiritual journey today, you remain a blessing to those you love and serve in their trials. And I want to encourage you to keep your eyes open and continue to press on in love.

Who Is My Neighbor?

All this talk of loving our neighbor begs the question, "Who is my neighbor?" Does Scripture mean my literal, living nearby, neighborhood neighbor?

The answer is yes, and no. Our neighbor is anyone we come into contact with in our daily life. Ever. It's your family, co-worker, church friend, former classmate, committee member, teacher, store clerk, homeless person, and yes, your literal neighbor across the street.

In the biblical context, everyone is your neighbor. And everyone in your life can benefit from a little more "neighborly" love.

Opportunity Knocks

Although we are called to love all our neighbors all the time, there's a unique opportunity to love our neighbor when they experience a time of trial in their life. Vulnerability brings with it an open door—one that often remains closed in the normal busyness of our lives. God intends for us to push open that door and step boldly into a person's life when they need it most.

There's a unique opportunity to love our neighbor when they experience a time of trial in their life.

We are meant to be part of the physical, human illustration of God's power. We are meant to help, heal, minister to, and love someone for His sake. And in the midst of brokenness, there's no better time to love our neighbor than the present.

No One Said It Would Be Easy

My friend Mallory likes to say, "Life isn't for sissies." I couldn't agree more. Every day life is hard. Either for us or for someone we care about.

- ✓ A cancer diagnosis
- ✓ Loss of a loved one
- ✓ Divorce
- ✓ Terminal illness
- ✓ Unemployment
- ✓ Foreclosure
- ✓ Surgery
- ✓ Long–term debilitation
- ✓ Financial crisis
- ✓ Parenting trials
- ✓ Aging parents or spouse
- ✓ Addiction

And the list goes on. We can be certain of one thing in this life: trials will come our way. As a Christian, I am comforted by the fact that Jesus knew a thing or two about hardship. Not only did he experience deep suffering, He warned us that we too would face trial at some point or another. "In this world you will have trouble," Jesus tells us. But thankfully He continues with this encouragement: "Take heart! I have overcome the world." (John 16:33 NIV)

Jesus doesn't want us to lose hope when tough circumstances block our path. He wants us to keep walking, even when we have to climb over the debris. And He promises to be right beside us. But what if the hardship affects someone you care about instead of you?

Uncertainty

In researching this book, I spoke to patients, to survivors, to family members, and to those who've helped others through dire circumstances. Many have looked straight into the eye of the cancer storm and lived through it. Some continue to live with a terminal diagnosis, trying to make the most of each day. Others I spoke to lost the person they loved most in this world.

Their stories of hardship are heartbreaking and real. More importantly, their stories have many similarities. I heard encouraging tales of extremely helpful people, as well as harrowing tales of those who were not so helpful.

People usually have good intentions, but intentions are often not enough. My desire for you is to eliminate intentions that never come to fruition or, worse, those that go awry. I don't want you to feel uncertain about helping someone in need. Ever. Again.

A Solution

Alongside will help you begin to unwrap the complex box of questions that arrives at your door the moment you hear "the news" and carry you through each step as you come alongside and bless others in need. This book is written for anyone who is on the outside looking in on another facing extreme trial. My express purpose is *to help you care for others* in their crisis, tragedy, long-term illness, or difficult situation.

Potential situations where *Alongside* will be useful:

✓ Your parent, brother, or sister was diagnosed with a long-term illness.
✓ Your sister-in-law's Mom passed away.
✓ Your friend was recently divorced.
✓ Your neighbor lost a child or spouse.
✓ Your church has a family encountering job loss or foreclosure.
✓ Your co-worker is caring for an aging parent.
✓ Your family member is having surgery.
✓ Your child's coach received a cancer diagnosis.

It doesn't matter the relationship or the circumstance, *Alongside* will become your trusted guidebook to help you walk with someone you know through their pain and love them along the way. By following the practical suggestions found within, I have no doubt you will become equipped to be a better friend, supporter, and warrior for God, especially when the hard times come.

May *Alongside* be only the beginning of your journey to love your neighbor with life-giving hope and encouragement during their greatest time of need.

Chapter 2

it's not about you

Above all else, guard your heart,
for everything you do flows from it.
—Proverbs 4:23 NIV

i have a secret to tell you. Stop what you're doing. Pay attention and listen closely. This secret is delicate and might be difficult to hear, but I'm saying it so the people you care about who are facing trial don't have to.

It's not about you.

Take a moment to memorize those four simple words, because they will serve you well as you begin the journey of loving your neighbor. Maybe you're thinking, "How absurd, of course I know it's not about me!" Good for you. You are in the minority, because more folks than you realize act as if it is all about them. The people I interviewed who experienced great hardship, life-altering diagnoses, and loss all said, in one way or another, that one of the hardest things to manage was the people who supposedly wanted to help but somehow made it about themselves.

So before we go any further I want to encourage you to keep this important truth in the forefront of your mind: It's not about you! It's about the person you are trying to help.

It's not about you! It's about the person you are trying to help.

A New Perspective

As you begin to look at your friend in trial through this new lens—one solely focused on them—there are several key considerations to bear in mind.

First, try not to let your own feelings cloud the picture. Hear me when I say this is a hard road to navigate. We want to help others, but often we can't see past our own grief, our desire to be "in the know," or our need to be appreciated. In the process, we forget we are reaching out to help someone who is not operating at full capacity or in a sound frame of mind. If you focus on the feelings of the person facing trial more than your own, you will be off to a great start.

Second, give lots of grace—especially to the person who's directly facing the trial. Crisis can make people irrational. Emotions tend to run high. You probably need to look no further than your own family to remember a time when someone said or did something offensive in a time of trial. Forgiveness and understanding are in order. Oh, and not being offended by everything.

It's not about you.

Third, remember to keep your motivations for helping pure. It's unattractive to help someone because it looks good to others or it appears righteous. The person you're serving needs privacy, sensitivity, and humility from you, not to be the talk of the bus stop, church halls, or grocery store. Love is the essential ingredient.

Fourth, temper your enthusiasm. There's often a sense of urgency in those who are naturally inclined toward reaching out to others in trial, but we would do well to remember that there are many demands on the afflicted one as well, such as time or physical limitations. Some of us will need to take a step back and try to keep perspective. A three hour visit is probably not in order.

It's not about you.

Finally, be mindful of how you acknowledge the person's plight. This can be a slippery slope. As a general rule, it's important to acknowledge the situation when it first happens. Don't keep silent. Unless you're super close to the person, often a polite acknowledgement is all they need. But do be mindful of what you say. We'll cover determining relationship types and what to say in chapters to come.

After the initial acknowledgement, realize that the person doesn't want to always be defined by their circumstance or illness. In other words, they might not want to talk about it every time they see you on the soccer field or at church. They are trying to maintain some semblance of normalcy.

The decision of whether or not to acknowledge or ask about their current hardship can also be situational. Are you at church where there's a line of people waiting to talk to the person after the service or are you one-on-one in the grocery store or neighborhood? If it's church or another place where there's a crowd, wait for a different time. They likely have zero energy to keep track of who talked to them and who didn't. And while you might feel rude for not asking about the crisis when you meet them face to face, they might not want to rehash their plight in the spaghetti aisle or in front of their children. In general, think about how you can acknowledge it the first time without putting undue burden on the person who already has burden enough.

If you are still unsure, consider your motivation. If you are thinking more about what you want to know instead of how they feel in that moment, then you are apt to do the wrong thing. If you put their needs first, you will likely know how to handle each situation.

Remember, *it's not about you.*

Chapter 3

in the know

The only true wisdom is in knowing you know nothing.
—Socrates

When you first hear that someone you love is in crisis, you encounter many emotions. Depending on the situation or how well you know the person, you might feel sad, shocked, surprised, helpless, angry, or uncertain. Initially, you go through your own time of pain. But you also want to help ease that person's pain or express your love and concern.

One of the hardest things to do is put aside your own feelings and focus on the person in need. If you are not ready to do so, then you should wait until you have come to terms with the situation for yourself so your emotions aren't detrimental to the one you love.

For example, if your friend has just been diagnosed with cancer and you can't stop crying, don't go over to her house to "comfort" her. Wait until you have your emotions in check so that you can be supportive, not make her feel worse. If you're not ready, you run the risk of your good intentions having a negative effect. And if you've ever been in such a place, you know there's nothing worse than making things worse.

The Big Picture

Getting a handle on the big picture is useful before you begin your foray into loving a person in need. The following is an overview of what you need to know to help you get your footing before you cross the street or pick up the phone. In Part 2: Taking Action you will find detailed, practical actions for helping.

1. Know your place.

Knowing your place in the life of the person in crisis will help you know how to respond. The following list of questions might be of help as you do this.

- ✓ Does the person consider me a close friend?
- ✓ Are they an extended or immediate family member?
- ✓ What is my day-to-day context in their lives?
- ✓ Do I see them regularly?
- ✓ Are they part of a church family or in my church family?
- ✓ Do they have family living in close proximity?
- ✓ Are there circumstances hindering my involvement?

Once you begin to think about the answers to these questions you will start to feel the nudge to either get involved immediately or wait to determine the best way you can help. For the remainder of this book, we will refer to your level of relationship with the following categories:

>Tier 1: caregiver/close family or friend
>Tier 2: friend/neighbor/co-worker/church member/sports teams/shared interests or organizations
>Tier 3: acquaintance/friend or family-of-a-friend/knowledge by association
>Tier 4: infrequent interaction/don't know them personally/never met

As you considered the previous list of questions, you should find yourself falling into one of these tiers. As we move forward, I will suggest specific ways to help based on your level of relationship, especially as we dive into Part 2.

For now, it's important to recognize that you cannot force yourself into someone else's personal situation simply to make yourself feel better, especially if you have a Tier 3 or 4 relationship with them. However, as you begin to help in appropriate ways, your relationship to the person could change over time. Embark on your alongside journey with an open mind and a willing heart, letting God be your guide. And be okay with your tier.

If the shoe doesn't fit, don't try to shove your bare foot in the door. In general:

✓ Tier 1 or 2: You likely feel the need to help immediately because of your close relationship to the person. Pray and read this book to fortify your help.

✓ Tier 3 or 4: If you have reservations about reaching out, it's likely you aren't very close to the person. Be patient, pray, and keep reading. I believe you will discover an appropriate way to express your support.

2. Know the needs.

In any crisis situation, there are certain practical needs involved. Knowing what these needs are will help you find the best way you can serve. Some initial needs might be:

- ✓ Food
- ✓ Childcare
- ✓ Doctor appointments (rides, support)
- ✓ Chores/Household needs
- ✓ Errands
- ✓ Finances
- ✓ Communication/information dissemination
- ✓ Coordination of resources and help

Coordination of resources should be first priority. Topping the list of resources are meals, information dissemination, and coordinating offers of help. There are many tools you can use to facilitate these needs, and the initial time spent setting them up will pay huge dividends in the future. Depending on your relationship to the person or family, you might offer to put these tools in place.

In the initial onset of a crisis or an extended period of trial, the most acute need can often be managing all the wonderful people that want to help. This is a great problem to have, but it can also be an extremely stressful burden for the family/person who is in crisis. Any effort to streamline the outpouring of food, the offerings of support, or the desire for information should be made as an order of first importance. On the other hand, a lack of help could go unnoticed if someone isn't overseeing that needs are met. It is essential to get an infrastructure in place to alleviate the chaos and undue stress for the person/family. I recommend consulting with the affected party first, of course, but the legwork can easily be delegated to someone else. Additionally, having one main contact person simplifies things and minimizes questions.

One family I interviewed designated a friend as their "Chief Operating Officer" or COO. The COO's responsibility was to manage the needs of the family by coordinating the requests to help. Designating this gatekeeper allows the family to focus on critical, time-sensitive, or medical-related needs. It's also easier when people ask how they can help to refer them to the COO or to the resources already in place to deal with specific needs. This alleviates an unnecessary burden on those in crisis. The following tools are invaluable and will help include people such as co-workers, neighbors, or other Tier 3 acquaintances who otherwise might not know how to help.

Recommended tools for resource management:

✓ Caring Bridge Site (www.caringbridge.org)

Caring Bridge provides for the accurate dissemination of information, including an initial journal entry describing the "back story" and journal updates for future information. This gives the family control over what gets shared publicly. It also alleviates the burden often placed on close family or friends to provide information to others outside the inner circle. Interested parties can be given access to the Caring Bridge site and avoid the common problem of inaccurate third-party information and rumors.

✓ Take Them a Meal (www.takethemameal.com)

Take them a Meal is a web-based coordination tool for meal management. It's fast, easy, and free. The service sends email invitations to those you want to invite to participate and reminder emails if they sign up to bring a meal. It also allows you to input multiple meal needs on a given day. Take Them a Meal also has a blog with helpful tips and offers a meal shipping service if you don't live nearby.

✓ Care Calendar (www.carecalendar.org)

Care Calendar is a web-based system for organizing meals and/ or other help. It allows the creation of a personalized calendar for the individual or family including: meals, driving, childcare, errands, yard work, cleaning, rides to doctor, and anything else you need! Care Calendar also allows for updates in the form of a "blog" where the patient or affected party can share information with those who are signed up as volunteers. This is helpful in the case of surgeries, death in the family, caring for an aging parent, or even the birth of a child, situations where you might not need a long-term Caring Bridge site.

✓ Lotsa Helping Hands (www.lotsahelpinghands.com)

Lotsa Helping Hands is a web-based system that coordinates meals and other needs. From their site: "When people rally to help someone in their family or Community, Lotsa Helping Hands makes it easy for each person to know what to do and when." In my experience, this site takes a bit more time to set up in advance, but it's perfect for a school or neighborhood situation where larger group coordination is involved. You can choose to have your community designated as open or closed (invitation only)—which is a great privacy option if needed. The site is free to use and includes message boards, meal coordination, photos, events (like fundraisers), tasks, visits, and errands/driving. This all-encompassing site could prove especially useful as a centralized resource if you've been assigned the position of COO (Chief Operating Officer).

3. Know the person.

Each individual or family in crisis, no matter their distress, share common characteristics that are useful to consider. As supporters, our job is to put their needs first. How we love them during this time hinges on understanding where they are coming from, especially if we've not been there ourselves. Even if we've experienced a similar situation, it's dangerous to make comparisons.

In my conversations with those who've received help for one reason or another, many common themes emerged in their feedback. One of those was a desire to remind others who they are and what they need. Even though I myself have been privy to extended periods of disability where I was required to rely on the mercy, help, and support of countless individuals, hearing from others solidified the truths I discovered in my times of crisis.

It's easy to get caught up in our own motivations or agenda and forget why we're helping, and more importantly, *who* we're helping. I hope the following truths will be as enlightening to you as they were to me.

Common Truths for a Person Facing Trial
They are:

- ✓ Not thinking clearly
- ✓ Wary of being defined by an illness or title
- ✓ Uncomfortable accepting help
- ✓ Feeling out of control
- ✓ Hurting
- ✓ Struggling to accept a new reality
- ✓ Unlikely to "let you know what you can do"
- ✓ Unable to make you feel good

They desire:

- ✓ Manageable amounts of visits, gifts, food, expressions of support
- ✓ Respect
- ✓ Privacy
- ✓ Normalcy
- ✓ Their own timetable for healing/accepting their situation
- ✓ To be heard

They need *you* to:

- ✓ Be present
- ✓ Listen
- ✓ Come alongside
- ✓ Support those they love
- ✓ Guard your tongue
- ✓ Believe in them
- ✓ Not take offense
- ✓ Serve out of love

This is not an exhaustive list, but it touches on the heavy hitters! Use this as a starting point. Later chapters will address these areas and many others in detail.

The greatest gift you can give those you're helping is to consider how they might be feeling. This diminishes the possibility of hurt feelings or your participation ending because you didn't get the response you wanted or expected.

> *The greatest gift you can give those you're helping is to consider how they might be feeling.*

As a person of faith, this is the point when I feel the need to pray for the strength to put other's needs ahead of my own as I humbly step in to serve.

4. Know the guidelines.

Below is a quick-reference list of general guidelines to bear in mind when helping others. It is an overview of all the research I conducted and highlights those concepts that were addressed most often. *Alongside* contains specific chapters for many of the categories on this list because they require expanded information.

If you've just found out "the news," these guidelines will help you as you begin to walk alongside another:

- ✓ Do unto others as you would have them do unto you.
- ✓ It's not about you!
- ✓ Tread lightly.
- ✓ Know your place.
- ✓ Be present.
- ✓ Bring food.
- ✓ Check your motives.
- ✓ Operate in your area of ability/giftedness.
- ✓ Ask permission.
- ✓ Don't over-visit.
- ✓ Pace yourself.
- ✓ Offer specific helps.
- ✓ Pray.
- ✓ Give helpful gifts.
- ✓ Watch what you say!
- ✓ Keep your emotions in check. (Or leave them at home!)

5. Know the questions.

Before we move on to the meat of the book, ask yourself the following questions as a means of readying your mind and heart for the journey ahead. You might want to jot down your thoughts on the notes pages provided in the Appendix, then refer to them after future chapters have given you a better idea of how to be helpful.

1. What does the person need today?
2. What is the Holy Spirit asking me to do?
3. What are my motives in wanting to help?
4. What would I want in the same situation?
5. Do I have a similar experience to share that might be useful?
6. Are there ways to help/tasks to be done that don't require permission?
7. What is my relationship to the person? What Tier am I?
8. Is there someone closer to the situation who might know the current needs?
9. Where is the person in their faith journey?
10. Do I have a "Go-To" meal or specific talent/gifting I can share?
11. Is this a marathon (long–term illness, death, divorce) or a 5K (surgery, financial strain)?
12. Is the person in trial a man or woman? Are there gender-specific guidelines that I need to think about?

Now that you have a high-level overview of what your friend might be feeling and the questions to consider as you move forward, your thoughts are probably churning over how you can help. Let's get specific so you can begin expressing your love and support for those in need.

As you read, join the conversation on www.facebook.com/alongsidebook. I also hope you will "love" your book—highlighters, pens, pencils, crayons, and earmarked pages are encouraged!

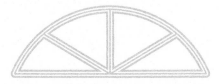

Part 2

taking action

And whatever you do, whether in word or
deed, do it all in the name of the Lord Jesus,
giving thanks to God the Father through him.
–Colossians 3:17 NIV

Chapter 4

go

The Lord turned to him and said, "Go in the
strength you have . . . Am I not sending you?"
–Judges 6:14 NIV

i t was a regular Wednesday afternoon in April when the phone rang. After a long, hard winter, the snow had melted away, and the kids were playing outdoors. The sun was finally shining, and we were basking in its rays, in the happiness warmth and light can bring.

And then my next-door neighbor called with horrible news. Our mutual neighbor, John, had died suddenly of a heart attack. In an instant, our world was enveloped in darkness. It was shocking.

I thought of his wife, Deborah, and her two precious sons tragically left without a husband and dad. I thought of John, with his compelling smile and his jolly, belly-rolling laughter. I pictured him playing catch with his son in the yard or opening the car door for his beautiful wife, dressed for an evening out.

Gone? I stood stunned.

Now's the time I'm supposed to do something, right?

I stared across the street at the perfectly manicured yard and the impeccably painted gray house with white trim. I had no idea what to do.

My neighbors and I commiserated, cried, and shared our disbelief. John had been out of state on a business trip when he died, so Deborah would be heading to the airport to get on a plane. I didn't have long to decide: stay home or go to her?

The Decision

I braved the 40 yards of concrete and knocked on Deborah's door. That walk across the cul-de-sac changed the trajectory not just of our relationship, but also my understanding of what people need in the face of hardship. It awakened an understanding of what it looks like to love your neighbor through some of life's most difficult circumstances. I've never regretted the decision to go.

When someone we care about gets bad news, we wonder if we should go to them. We wonder if the family is overwhelmed with people. We don't want to intrude. We convince ourselves we are not needed.

But there is power in internal promptings when it comes to making some decisions. If the first thought that crosses your mind is "go," then don't sit around hemming and hawing and worrying about what they will think of you if you show up at their doorstep. Because guess what? By acting on your instinct,

If you are feeling led to go, by all means, GO!

you will be the exception, not the rule. If you are feeling led to go, by all means, GO!

One friend who tragically lost a son to suicide described it like this: "The people who showed up were the most brave. Next were those who called. We recognized and appreciated the courage it took for those people to reach out."

Most people are afraid of how they might be perceived or of their own discomfort with the situation. (Say it with me: "It's not about you!") These feelings keep them running away from the storm instead of directly into it. In a blog post on michelecushatt.com titled "How to Bring Relief to Those Who Grieve," author Michele Cushatt writes, "We're often more concerned about securing our own comfort than offering it to the one who needs it most."

Even though you worry what they'll think, they likely aren't thinking about you right now! They may not even remember later that you came. And that's okay, too.

Still unsure? Evaluating your relationship with the person by the Tier system will help you determine if going is a good way for you to take action. The "go" option is best suited for those with a Tier 1 or Tier 2 relationship, unless of course you've been in the same situation.

My best advice:

✓ Tier 1: Yes! Go!
✓ Tier 2: Pray and discern the closeness of your relationship with the person before showing up on a doorstep. Ask yourself, "Am I uniquely qualified or feeling particularly led?"
✓ Tier 3 or 4: Going is probably not the best way for you to love your neighbor.

If you are in Tier 2, 3 or 4 and are feeling led to go, consider asking permission before you show up. Text or call. Say something like, "I'd like to come by if you're up to it." Or "I'd love to be with you right now if you want." Even "I'm on my way unless I hear otherwise from you" is helpful.

No matter what Tier you fall into, if you are overly emotional about the person's news and/or are so deeply affected by the person's trial you risk being a distraction to the ones you're trying to support, I recommend you stay home until such time as you are able to control your sorrow and be comforting or helpful. Otherwise, trust in God's power, say a prayer for guidance, and get moving.

When in doubt . . . Go!

Chapter 5

respect their journey

Let each of you look not only to his own
interests, but also to the interests of others.
–Philippians 2:4 ESV

during the five years my best friend Kelley battled cancer, we had an unspoken agreement to walk on Wednesdays. Whether we walked on the track or treadmill, in the neighborhood or around the lake, if it was Wednesday and we were able, we were walking. This was *our* time. We did everything we could to preserve it. *We needed it.*

Over those years, she endured extensive, repeated cancer treatments, and I had four back surgeries. As you can imagine, these circumstances affected our ability to walk on any given Wednesday.

The beauty of our challenging situations was our willingness to do whatever it took to help the other continue. If she couldn't walk fast, we would do the treadmill instead of the track, each at our own pace, side by side. When the roles were reversed, it was my turn to plod along while she walked energetically on the machine next to me, even if she'd rather have been doing a different workout. And if one of us were completely incapacitated (which was too often the case!), we would fill that time slot with something entirely different. Our favorite was to skip the workout and sit in the hot tub at the gym. Oh, yeah, and then lunch.

In those years of walking with Kelley wherever and however we could, I learned the importance of respecting someone's journey, of meeting them where they are—even if that place is at the expense of our own agenda for the day.

For Kelley and me, this went far beyond our habit of working out. It also infiltrated our conversations and other time spent together. There were times I knew she didn't want to spend even a minute talking about sickness, treatments, logistics, plans, or feelings. But other days we needed to "go there." In those moments, I needed to respect her desires all the more, remaining focused on her circumstance and how I could help her through it.

Depending on the particular trial, you can respect your friend's or loved one's difficult journey in any of the following ways.

Don't Try to Fix It

The lesson of respecting a person's journey applies to one of the most challenging aspects of helping someone through a trial: our desire to "fix" the person or their circumstances. Remember, it's not your journey. It's theirs. Even the most well-meaning folks have done more harm than good by asserting a "fix-it" mentality. (We will talk more about this in Chapter 10: Listen Well.)

Honor Their Privacy

This is the single most valuable lesson I learned about caring for others through hardship.

My friend Kelley's fight was a long one. She had countless setbacks amidst the blessing of the extra years we had with her beyond her original prognosis. Her family was a vital part of our church family and our local community, which meant many people were involved in caring for them. This brought both good and bad circumstances. On the one hand, they were well cared for and supported by a plethora of amazing and helpful people. On the other, her situation was very public, and it was hard to maintain their privacy.

Everyone always wanted to know how Kelley, the kids, and her husband were doing. They wanted to know what the family needed. What happened in the latest treatment or procedure. What they could do to help.

To maintain communication with others while protecting the family from receiving all the inquiries became an exhausting but necessary task. To help with this, we established a Caring Bridge site and diligently updated the thousands of folks who followed Kelley's cancer journey. Because of my (unidentified at the time) job as COO (Chief Communications Officer), I often put out prayer requests, rallied the troops, updated the site, etc.

In the beginning, I always sought permission from Kelley's family first—requesting input, asking what they wanted me to post, do, or say. There were never any major issues that I knew of, until *that day.*

Roughly three years into Kelley's five-year battle, her cancer came back. I was one of the first to find out the news and went into autopilot. I sent a message to the church prayer chain, which was a regular duty I'd had before, asking people to pray as Kelley's family faced yet another setback.

The specifics aren't important. What is important is this: I forgot to ask her permission to put this request on the prayer chain. And in the process, I hijacked what little privacy my dear friend had left.

When she called that day, I could tell something was wrong, which was not typical. Kelley was the most loving, considerate, kind, soft-spoken, witty, and funny woman I knew. I had never been in a position to experience her disappointment.

And that's what it was. Disappointment. There was no anger, no harsh words, just a soft-spoken, kind-as-possible delivery. "I wish you hadn't shared this new development with the prayer chain. I really wasn't ready for everyone to know yet. I wanted it to stay private for now."

Ugh.

I was devastated that in the midst of the most awful trial a person can face, *I made it worse.* I apologized profusely. Full of shame and remorse, I was crushed that I had wounded my friend and robbed her of what little control she did have in her life—when, how, and *if* she would share her situation with others.

Ever full of grace and love, my sweet friend forgave me immediately. And she never mentioned it again.

> *Don't share what's not yours to share.*

Hard as it was, the lesson I learned that day has served me well ever since. And I pray it will be a warning to you: tread lightly, don't share what's not yours to share, and always remember—it's not about you.

Honor Their Physical Limitations

If you typically worked out together, and they can't exercise any longer, find out what they can do and do that instead. To love them well through their difficult time, it's essential to honor them in this way. This could mean getting in your own workout another way or at another time, changing a routine or time slot, or making concessions (such as how fast or how often) on your activity. When you put your friend first (or put yourself in her walking or non-walking shoes), you will quickly see how valuable this shift is to her.

Maybe working out isn't her thing, but shopping is! Offer to take your friend to the mall, then get the fancy electric wheelchair and walk beside her. Or if she can't get out of the house at all, bring a fun adventure in—such as a picnic, a movie night, a manicure/pedicure session, or a hairdresser. Help them feel like they are experiencing everyday things, even if they can't go out.

Help Them Accept Their New Identity

He was perfectly healthy; now he's a cancer patient. She was happily married; now she is a widow, divorcee, or single parent. He was a thriving employee; now he's disabled. She was a mom or mom-to-be; now she's part of the "I've lost a child" club.

When the world all of a sudden gives us a new label, we need help dealing with that new reality, whatever it may be. Be sensitive to these new identities in your conversations, so you don't unintentionally hurt or offend.

Help Maintain Their Dignity

So many people have said to me, "I want to be treated as a person, not an illness."

People need you to love them for who they are, not because of their hardship. It doesn't benefit them to feel like they are your charity case, that you only care about them because they are ill or

People need you to love them for who they are, not because of their hardship.

in need. Don't let pity rule the day here, folks. It will only cause your friend to feel worthless and resentful, which I know is not your intent.

Give Them Time

There is nothing worse than being rushed through your feelings by someone else. If you've ever lost a loved one, you understand. There comes a time when the world wants you to move on, but you are still grieving. There's a very real loneliness born from holding missing pieces to a puzzle that everyone close to you wants put back in place—a puzzle that will likely remain unfinished for a long time. In fact, it may never be whole again.

Similarly, a new diagnosis requires time to adjust to before being bombarded with requests, even if the requests are well intentioned or necessary. Move slowly, cautiously. If your friend is injured or recovering from surgery or illness, don't put your timetable on their healing. Every person's body is different. Just because someone else you know healed after two weeks doesn't mean this person should, will, or can. Be patient. Respect that they will not heal on your timetable.

Additionally, if you are waiting for a response from them, expect to wait longer than normal. Remember, your friend's life has changed profoundly, maybe for a limited time or possibly forever. You might have to wait.

Give Them Space

When someone is in the middle of a crisis, the last thing we want is to contribute an additional burden. When my sister's husband was sick, she received lots of phone calls from friends and family, and it became a challenge to find time to play back her answering machine messages (voicemail). After she heard the messages, she felt obliged to call people back, which became another hardship, even if she *did* want to talk.

If you're calling someone to express concern and want to leave a message, be sure to clarify that you aren't expecting a return call. Give them permission to call only if they want to talk, then they won't feel added pressure to get more done when they're already maxed out. If you're calling about something that requires a response, suggest that you will call back another time.

Like phone calls, texts can also be overwhelming because they seem to demand a reply. If you text, clarify that you don't need to hear back. A text can be intrusive—especially if they're using that method to communicate with close family and friends. If you're Tier 1, text is okay. If you're Tier 2, you might text or call, but convey you don't need a reply.

For Tier 3 and Tier 4 relationships, one option is to use the Caring Bridge site to express your condolences or well wishes. Another good way to acknowledge your concern or sympathy is with a card or note sent through the mail or a message sent via email. With these methods, the person can decide when they want to read and if they want to reply.

All these methods of reaching out allow you to express your concern but also allow the person to process the situation in their own way without further obliging them to handle even more in a time of chaos.

Ask Their Permission

This is rule number one, especially if you are in a position where others are turning to you for information or ways to help. Find a way to ask the affected party's permission before sharing information or suggesting ways people can help. If I had asked Kelley's permission before I shared her health setback, I would have easily and successfully avoided disappointing and hurting my friend.

Another time I made a mistake in this area was after a neighbor passed away. Another neighbor and I were trying to be helpful to a house now full of single men, so we decided to organize the leftovers and clean out the refrigerator. Apparently our version of what was still edible differed greatly from theirs, and unwittingly we threw away some things very precious to those guys. This simple example illustrates how we crossed the line by not asking permission before acting. They sweetly mentioned the error of our ways the next day and asked us to please refrain from disposing of food they were looking forward to eating!

There are times when one doesn't need permission to do a nice thing. For example, if you want to send a card, write an email, send a gift, purchase groceries, etc., you often don't need to ask the person's permission in advance for these specific acts of kindness.

Areas to seek permission include visiting (especially in light of a long-term or terminal illness), sensitive informational matters (such as prayer requests or publishing their private information), making plans for them, putting their name on anything (a race/benefit/run/fundraiser), changing their schedule, caring for their kids, or any other more personal request—like throwing away leftovers!

Think Before You Act

As a general rule, think before you do anything, especially if your emotions are running high. Focus on your friend or loved one and keep your eyes on their needs. To decipher what is helpful, questions like "What might I like in this similar situation?" or "Do I have any experience in this area?" or "Could what I'm about to do bring harm or any negative repercussions?" are good to ask yourself.

Refer back to the "Know the questions" section of Chapter 3: In the Know for more to consider before you act.

Be Authentic

Authenticity stands out like a rainbow in the height of a storm. If you are helping out of obligation or guilt, the person you are trying to serve will likely sense your masked motivations. If you cannot be genuine in your efforts to help, express care or concern, or show sympathy, then don't.

Going through a trial is a deep and vulnerable journey. The last thing you want is to add to someone's pain by making them feel like a charity case. Authenticity demands serving with humility, not seeking recognition or affirmation. True service is that which doesn't look for acknowledgement or thanks.

One friend told me it was hard for her "when people talked about serving me to everyone they knew." I'd caution you against waving your service as a banner for all to see in hopes of receiving praise. Sadly, I'm guilty as charged. There have been times I've delivered a meal and then rushed to tell my friends about it. I'm not proud of that, but I'm working on serving without mentioning it to others.

When you humbly and genuinely serve, you will bless the receiver, not glorify yourself.

When you humbly and genuinely serve, you will bless the receiver, not glorify yourself.

Obey Their Guidelines

Ben from Rwanda had this valuable insight about well-meaning friends who thought they were the exception to the rule. "It was unhelpful when people wouldn't listen or thought the rules we put in place didn't apply to them, such as 'we are not accepting visitors,' 'please only contact Ben or Megan' (a friend who operated as our Chief Operating Officer), or 'don't talk about specifics in front of our kids.'"

Guidelines are put in place for a reason, even if you don't understand it. Disobeying the family's guidelines might not be intentional, but it can produce unwanted outcomes for the person or family you're helping. And you never want to unwittingly add more stress to an already challenging situation.

Adhering to someone's wishes is a huge blessing, even if it's difficult. And in doing so, you keep the focus on your neighbor and express unconditional love when they need it most.

Chapter 6

offer specific help

Carry each other's burdens, and in this
way you will fulfill the law of Christ.
–Galatians 6:2 NIV

W hen I was pregnant with our third child, my husband, Craig, and I began attending a parenting class offered through our church. The class started just before I was sentenced to my bed for 11 weeks to prevent my youngest from being born too early. We initially thought we'd have to drop out of the class because I couldn't leave the house. I was only allowed to go down the stairs once a day. And this wasn't a short class, folks. It lasted 18 weeks!

I was so worried about the little bun in my oven that hadn't finished cooking, I couldn't have told you which end was up. I had an intensely busy, traveling husband and two kids, ages four and two. And my whole family lived in Wisconsin, six hours away. I was new to this church and this state. My in-laws were our only family nearby, and they were already doing more than their fair share to help.

When we told our leaders we'd have to drop out of the class, they offered to hold the class in our basement so we could continue to attend, and one of the women in our group offered to bring a meal each Sunday to class so we'd have dinner for the following night.

Every Sunday until I was set free, our newfound friends piled into my messy basement (I couldn't clean up, I could barely make it down the stairs for goodness sake!) so I could lie on the couch for the videos and discussion. If it hadn't been for the leaders' generous offer, we'd have dropped out. That class enlightened and impacted our parenting for years to come, and it came with a generous and cherished side benefit of life-long friendships.

These two specific offers—meeting in our home and dinner each week— were worth their weight in gold to my family at a time when we were rubbing mere pennies together.

"Let Me Know What I Can Do"

Acts 20:35 says, "It is more blessed to give than to receive." After living through bed rest during my pregnancy and five surgeries—all with three children under the age of eight—I coined a new phrase: "It is harder to receive than to give."

If you've been on the receiving end of kindness in the face of hardship or tragedy, I think you will agree. If you haven't, it's difficult to appreciate the feeling, but please take the following to heart.

When it comes to helping others, there are three things you need to know:

1. People don't like to be in need of help.
2. A generic offer ("Let me know what I can do.") is supremely unhelpful.
3. Specific offers of help allow you to combat both of these problems.

Hear me when I say that the person you are trying to help will be challenged by the mere notion of accepting help, especially if that person is a woman. Don't call the ACLU on me, but this has been true in my research and experience—most men will take all the help you can give, knowing they need it. Women, on the other hand, will be much more hesitant, as if needing your help means they are lacking or inadequate in some way. As those who want to love amidst the hardest circumstances of life, we must counteract this feeling at all costs. A woman's welfare depends on it.

> *Specific offers of help allow you to assist the person in need while at the same time making it easier for the person to say yes to your help.*

Specific offers of help allow you to assist the person in need while at the same time making it easier for the person to say yes to your help. Specific offers also give the person the power to say no if they need space, time, or just don't want that help in that moment.

Before we get into the specific kinds of help we can offer, it is also important to note the one wretched, useless phrase spoken by well-intentioned people: "Let me know what I can do."

These words put the entire burden back on the affected party. The person in need is not likely to ever actually tell you "what you can do." It's almost impossible in a crisis or life-altering situation to think about what you need, much less remember who offered to help!

The person in need is not likely to ever actually tell you "what you can do."

My friend Dan from Minnesota said it well: "The good intentions are there, but that phrase transfers the burden back to the receiver, and most likely the receiver will never request, so nothing ever gets given."

Additionally, those well-intentioned words can cause undue stress. After losing her infant son, Astrid from Texas said, "It was stressful when people asked, 'What can I do to help?' I sometimes felt I had to give people tasks to help them feel useful."

Remember, this person in crisis is not really fired up about needing your help in the first place, which makes it even more difficult for them to "tell you what you can do."

Ben from Rwanda had a wife battling brain cancer. He said:

The people who best helped me were the people who helped me with something specific—doing our laundry, cleaning our home, watching our kids, giving financially, meeting, or talking. Most of these folks did this on a regular basis, so I could count on them and didn't need to worry about scheduling others or navigating changes. This was a huge help and alleviated a lot of stress for me. Others offered something specific that was a one-time thing but was a huge help for our family, like experiences for our family to enjoy together in the midst of the chaos.

So what kinds of specific help should we offer?

Offer to Take a Specific Role

One way to make the generic more meaningful is to offer to take on a specific role in the continued care/recovery/healing. If you are Tier 1, you might be the perfect candidate for one of the following options.

Ben and his wife, Susie, who shared their wisdom with me for this book, explained that they designated a close friend to be the COO (Chief Operating Officer), in charge of managing all the resources, people, tasks, communications, and family needs after Susie was diagnosed with brain cancer. This title and position is something I hadn't thought of before, but believe to be invaluable, along with several other key Tier 1 or 2 roles.

- **Chief Operating Officer:** Manage/oversee all resources, people, tasks, communications and needs, and act as the primary liaison for the family/individual when needed/asked.
- **Communications Director:** Manage or set up information dissemination to large groups/churches/schools/community via resources like Caring Bridge or email lists.
- **Specific needs/Calendar Planner:** Manage errands/rides/kids' schedules/needs/tasks for the family or individual.
- **Caregiver Liaison:** Manage childcare, post-surgical care, or in-home helpers.
- **Meal Coordinator:** Manage meal offers/delivery/dates/details and coordinate between different interest groups that might include church, school, work, clubs, neighborhood, family and/or close friends.
- **Advice Collector:** Receive and discern any insights, suggestions, offers, treatments, medical or other information that might overwhelm a family/individual. When the time is appropriate, present any useful, necessary information, allowing the family/individual to focus on more pressing matters.
- **Prayer Warrior Coordinator:** Coordinate/plan all things prayer related, including but not limited to prayer meetings, hourly prayer times, specific prayer events like for surgery

or key milestones, and/or update prayer chains the family/individual specifies.

✓ **Chief Appointment Coordinator:** Organize rides to doctor appointments, chemotherapy/radiation, errands or any other place needed.

Offer to Do Specific Tasks

If you are not in a position to help in a specific role, consider offering to help with specific tasks. Take note that there might be a resource in place to coordinate some items on this list. If not, consider coordinating them! These options are great for those folks in Tier 2 or 3 relationships.

✓ Errands
✓ Grocery shopping
✓ Yard work/gardening
✓ House cleaning
✓ Pet care
✓ House care/sitting
✓ Rides to appointments (consistently is best)
✓ Meals
✓ Fundraising
✓ Driving children
✓ Childcare
✓ Daily activities/chores
✓ Visits
✓ Meal clean up
✓ Laundry
✓ Breakfast or lunch, especially if they are home alone recovering or their spouse is traveling.
✓ Use of your car or house for their visiting family/friends

These suggestions give you a way to change the generic "let me know what I can do" to a tangible "this is what I can do." And that, my friends, is a huge blessing in a time of need.

An even better solution is to change the phrase slightly.

- "I'd love to _____, if it's alright with you."
- "I'm here if you need _____."
- "I'll check in to see if and when you need _____."
- "Think it over, and I'll check back with you to see if you are ready for help with _____."
- "I have _____ , and I'm happy to have you use it."

Dan from Minnesota likens making a specific offer to choosing a birthday gift. He said, "If the giver can figure out the perfect gift—or at least make a solid effort—that is 1,000 times better than if I need to make a 'list' so you can get me something." The same goes for helping those you care about in their time of need.

Specific offers of a task show you mean business, and they demonstrate your genuine desire to help. Otherwise your words are just an empty phrase that won't impact anyone.

Offer to Run Specific Errands

When you don't know what to do or how to help, especially if you're in a Tier 2 or 3 relationship with the person in need, try offering to run errands for them. The list below provides some ideas for where to start:

- ✓ Library
- ✓ Pet store
- ✓ Dry cleaners
- ✓ Post office
- ✓ Pharmacy

✓ Home improvement store
✓ Grocery store
✓ Sporting goods store
✓ Dog groomer

If you're in Tier 1 or 2, consider replacing social activities you might have enjoyed regularly together, like coffee, lunch, or shopping, with an offer of doing something productive—and equally helpful—instead.

Offer What You're Already Doing

Another way you might be more likely to get a "yes" from the person you want to help is by offering to do something for the person that you are already doing. Think about what you need to accomplish in a given week and offer to do those same things for someone going through a trial. Start with the list from the previous section if you need ideas. The point is, if you're already doing it, it's easier for the person in need to accept your help without feeling like they've burdened you.

Angie from Minnesota has spent years living out double difficulties—her own cancer diagnosis and a son with Type I diabetes. With these intense trials, she was the recipient of a myriad of help. She said, "I had a friend that would email or text whenever she was going to Target, Costco, the grocery store, etc. and ask what she could pick up for me. I often took her up on it, as I felt like I wasn't asking her for anything 'extra'—she was going to those places anyway."

I have found this to be an easy way to help, especially when you don't have time for something big or extra. You might think going to Costco for someone is pretty big, but if you're there anyway, it's not as hard as it sounds.

Susie from Rwanda is fully on board with this concept, too. She said, "Instead of saying, 'let me know if you want me to do your grocery shopping' and expecting me to do that, send a text from the grocery store that says, 'I'm at the store, what can I pick up for you?'" In other words, the recipient of your offer is more likely to take you up on it if you are already there. Which is what you want! If someone says no the first time, keep on offering. It might take time before they know you are genuinely willing.

I remember when a neighbor who I didn't know very well was in the midst of her recovery from breast cancer surgery. I was not able to help her as often as I would have liked, so I tried to find small ways to help when I could. I had made her dinner a few times, and we had shared contact information. Originally, this was definitely a Tier 4 relationship, but through small gestures I had moved into Tier 3. (Not that we are striving to "move up." This information is to provide context.)

One day she came to mind while I was at the grocery store, which was just down from Keva Juice, a frozen drink shop. I remembered my friend Kelley's dependence on smoothies after she had endured chemotherapy and found it hard to eat or swallow. I knew Kelley's order by heart because I brought Keva to her regularly. With a prompting of what I believe to be the Holy Spirit, I decided to text my neighbor and specifically offer to bring her something from Keva Juice.

At first she was reluctant. She said she didn't want me to make a special trip and had no idea what she'd want. I said, "I'm here anyway. I will send you the link to their menu, and you can choose what you like. Text me your order, and it would be my pleasure to deliver it as I'm going right past your house to take my groceries home anyway."

I had given her a way to say yes by removing the obstacles of guilt and doubt. The offer wasn't "I'd love to help you, what do you need?" The offer was "I'm already here, and I'd love to do this for you." It's all in the presentation. Remember, we're dealing with people in need who don't want to be a bother. Our job is to shine a tiny light in their darkest spaces, and sometimes that little sliver of sunshine comes in a Styrofoam cup with a straw.

Offer Help During a Visit

When I was recovering from my spinal fusion surgery, I endured a very challenging time emotionally. I had to stay on the pain pills much longer than I wanted. They made me aggravated, short-tempered, and grumpy with the people around me. I didn't realize how depressed I was until I was on the other side of my three-month recovery and felt better again.

One morning during those dark days, my sweet friend Deborah showed up to bring me oatmeal. I could get around, walk to the bathroom, sit in a chair and all that, but I couldn't carry anything heavier than a plate or cup. I felt like a bystander in my own life. I spent lots of time home alone since my husband was at work and the kids were at school. I was pretty lonely.

But Deborah delivered more than oatmeal that day. She also served up a willing heart. She sat in my "visitor chair" and chatted as I ate that warm bowl of love doused with raisins and sugar. And then she said some magic words.

"How about if I change your sheets? There's really nothing like clean sheets when you're stuck in your bed all day."

Any sense of embarrassment was quickly replaced by the slow smile that grew on my lips. "I would absolutely love clean sheets. Thank you."

On we chatted as she unraveled my bed linens and renewed not just my sheets but my spirits too. I never imagined what a loving and thoughtful gesture crisp, clean sheets could be. Ever since, whenever I am able, I pay that sweet kindness forward. And when I do, I think of my angel, Miss Deborah, who now has angels in heaven for friends.

Angie from Minnesota also loved "productive visits." She said,

Coming over for a "visit" then helping fold a load of laundry or unloading the dishwasher, changing the sheets, or wiping off counters while you are there and visiting is a great way to help.

I think most people are hesitant to ask for help and are more likely to 'let' a friend come over for some girl or guy time—which can then lead to help with household tasks rather than having to ask specifically for that help.

Come Alongside for Difficult Tasks

There are endless heart-wrenching, challenging, and just plain yucky tasks people face in the midst of trials. Your goal is to come alongside and make these challenges more bearable.

My neighbor Deborah was diagnosed with breast cancer just two years after her husband died from a heart attack. During her cancer treatments, when she started to lose her hair en masse, another neighbor and I offered to shave Deborah's head. It's a little disconcerting to go to a salon for this type of "beauty treatment." We wanted her to have privacy—and camaraderie. We decided to make it as fun as possible with coffee, scones, and a razor. Our private bathroom party of three was a sweet reminder of the blessings in trial as we managed to laugh amidst falling tears and chunks of hair.

Kris, a former cancer patient, said, "I had a friend go with me to buy a wig. This was a great help because I felt overwhelmed at the thought of going alone." In my estimation, there is nothing more precious than coming alongside a loved one in their very challenging circumstance and offering to join in, because as I mentioned earlier, they aren't likely to take you up on the "let me know what I can do" offer. Your job is to think of the challenging tasks they might be faced with and offer practical and specific help.

Consider these options of offering help that might make it easier for them to allow you to come alongside:

- "I can go along if you need to choose a dress for the funeral." Or "I can help you pick out clothes for your kids."

- "I have experience writing obituaries. Would you like me to get you started?"
- "I can help write thank you notes."
- "Would you like a ride to _____?"

It's important you recognize these suggestions as a means to being helpful and useful without making them feel incapable. When your whole life is out of control, you want to be able to do something for yourself. So joining them where they are is far better than stripping them of their independence.

Remember, come *alongside*!

If you sense they are overwhelmed or the timing isn't right, you might offer to take on a task entirely. But please, tread lightly. You never know what "task" might be of monumental importance to them at that moment. Don't undermine their feelings by saying, "You don't need to do that, I can do it for you." There is a fine line between helpful and overpowering, so be sure to check your bossy clipboard at the door. Choose your words wisely and speak in love.

Here's a list of daunting tasks you might offer to do alongside a friend in specific circumstances:

Death of a loved one:
✓ Shop for funeral clothes
✓ Notify family/friends
✓ Take care of deceased's belongings
✓ Clean out rooms/closets
✓ Write obituary
✓ Write funeral thank you notes
✓ Order funeral flowers
✓ Answer phone calls
✓ Organize finances

✓ Notify credit cards/banks/memberships of deceased's status
✓ Organize prayer service
✓ Create photo boards
✓ Plan funeral/memorial service
✓ Make funeral arrangements
✓ Coordinate meals/receptions/gatherings of family/friends
✓ Prepare house for guests
✓ Answer emails/inquiries
✓ Help move/remodel
✓ Write Caring Bridge updates
✓ Run errands

Cancer/long-term illness:
✓ Plan/coordinate prayer service
✓ Answer phone calls
✓ Notify family/friends
✓ Write Caring Bridge (or similar) updates
✓ Purchase specific items (i.e. wigs, scarves, wheelchairs, hospital beds)
✓ Prepare house for absence during hospital stay
✓ Pack for surgery/hospital stay
✓ Plan care for family/needs
✓ Create health care directives
✓ Prepare will/child custody directives
✓ Organize scrapbook/home movies
✓ Schedule photo shoot
✓ Transcribe letters to family/loved ones
✓ Prepare/freeze meals
✓ Clean/organize house
✓ Manage children's activities/school/sports
✓ Help with exercise or physical rehabilitation

Divorce:

- ✓ Attend hearings
- ✓ Fill out legal paperwork
- ✓ Help with legal obligations
- ✓ Help with move/remodel
- ✓ Help with routine tasks formerly handled by spouse
- ✓ Drive/help with children
- ✓ Accompany to social events
- ✓ Accountability for exercise
- ✓ Household chores

These lists will help you start to focus on the less obvious or "fun" needs your friend might have. Another way to recognize the more difficult tasks is by thinking of those things you don't like to do alone on a regular day, then offering to come alongside the person in trial to accomplish those tasks.

Let Their No be No

There are times even our best and most specific offers of help will not be accepted. It's right to offer, but you have to allow the person you're

> *Allow the person you're helping to be clear about what they need and don't need.*

helping to be clear about what they need and don't need. If you have a Tier 2, 3, or 4 relationship, there are certain offers a person might not feel comfortable accepting from you. Remember, it's not about you. If you're not convinced, reread Chapter 5: Respect Their Journey.

Susie from Rwanda gives her opinion on this subject:

Help often feels like obligation. I appreciated everyone's offers to help, and I knew I needed it, but taking people up on it was often difficult to execute. If they want to clean my house, that's so sweet, but then I need to get out of bed and describe what I need. The person who wants to do my laundry is an angel, but I need to be organized enough to get all of my dirty stuff in one place at the right time.

Even the most generous of offers can be a hassle for the person you want to bless. So if they say no, you need to honor that response. As per Susie's advice, I would clarify that if you're a Tier 1 friend/family, you will likely be in a better position to offer helps that are perhaps harder for someone to execute who doesn't know the family or person intimately.

Not long ago, I had a Tier 3 relationship with a woman facing a recurrence of breast cancer. She called to ask me a favor regarding her son, and I tried to offer her specific additional help during our conversation. She was very clear with me that she was covered in that area, and I didn't know her well enough to insist.

I had to allow her no to be no and not push my agenda on her. Not helping can be a challenging feat sometimes, but it can also be a great way to be helpful! A lot of emotional energy can go into defending a position. You don't want the person you're helping to waste their precious energy on you.

As evidenced throughout this chapter, there are countless specific ways to help those you care about who are facing trial. When you recognize that people are not keen on receiving help or cannot respond to your offer of "let me know what I can do," you will skip the empty words and offer up life-giving, tangible ways to help instead.

Chapter 7

be present

*The friend who can be silent with us in a moment
of despair or confusion, who can stay with us in an
hour of grief and bereavement, who can tolerate not
knowing, not curing, not healing and face with us the
reality of our powerlessness, that is a friend who cares.*
–Henri J.M. Nouwen, *Out of Solitude*

t he Book of Job in the Bible tells the story of how Job lost
everything—his livelihood, his children and grandchildren, his
vast wealth, his health. During his profound pain and mourning,
his three friends traveled far from their own lands to give comfort
and sympathy.

These friends joined him in sackcloth and ashes in the dirt and demonstrated what it looks like to be present: "And they sat with him on the ground seven days and seven nights, and no one spoke a word to him, for they saw that his suffering was very great." (Job 2:13 ESV)

Now I'm not saying that Job's three friends are models for us once they opened their mouths. (They were less than encouraging during his subsequent trials.) But for at least seven days, they did the right thing. They sat with Job and participated in his suffering.

For seven days, they came alongside.

My close friend Gary became the primary caretaker for my friend Deborah when she faced terminal cancer. During her last months of life at home, he was in the trenches day in and day out, caring for her selflessly. He created perfect meals to her standards and ever-changing requests, changed the sheets, made doctor and hospice appointments, helped her get to the bathroom without falling, monitored visitors and requests.

In the midst of his focus on Deborah, he told me he doesn't remember what people said, he just remembers they were there. His favorite quote is, "If you see someone crying, don't just do something, stand there!" Sometimes the best way to express we care is our presence.

Presence as an Action

Over and over again in research and conversations, people expressed that the most helpful thing people "did" for them was simply to be with them. We think we have to *do* something, but presence is a powerful action of its own. The one who shows up stands out.

> *The one who shows up stands out.*

Consider these quotes about the value of presence from people who've experienced all kinds of trials.

- Kris, a breast cancer survivor: "Do be there, if only to hold your friend or loved one's hand for a little while. Whether it's during a chemo session, sitting in a radiation waiting room, or waiting for a doctor to share test results, the power of human touch is amazing and can certainly be a gift during these times."

- Rita, a former licensed psychologist who faced her son's suicide and the loss of her husband: "Sometimes you just have to show up. What I want you to do is join with me, not look at me with sympathy. "

- Sandra from Minnesota, speaking of dear friends who took turns stopping by with Starbucks during her divorce: "Sometimes we talked, sometimes we prayed, but most of the time, they were just still and near to me. I will never forget how the loss was lessened by their love."

- Claire, a 14-year-old from Minnesota who lost her brother: "The best thing was people who just came over and sat. Quietly. No words. No stupid platitudes, because there was literally nothing that they could say that would make it better. They were just there. And later, after the first few days, they came over again to watch movies and TV and play Xbox."

- Stephanie from New Mexico, whose daughter who was born six weeks early and spent a week in the NICU (Neonatal Intensive Care Unit): "A friend of mine came to the NICU every day. I was so distraught I barely spoke. She would bring me lunch and say nothing. She would just sit and be by my side or watch TV. It was wonderful. She was a Godsend during that time, and I will never forget her gift of love."

- Jenny, a hospice nurse who lost two special patients in three weeks and her uncle and grandma a month later: "The biggest help to me during that time was my dear friends who were there and spent time with me. Nobody said any brilliant words that made me feel so much better, but my friends walked with me as I went through the valley of grief. More than anything, we all just want someone to be there. Be."

There is power in being present. Catherine Woodiwiss speaks about it this way in her Sojourner.net article "A New Normal: 10 Things I've Learned about Trauma":

There is a curious illusion that in times of crisis people "need space." I don't know where this assumption originated, but in my experience, it is almost always false. Trauma is a disfiguring, lonely time, even when surrounded in love; to suffer through trauma alone is unbearable. Do not assume others are reaching out, showing up, or covering all the bases. It is a much lighter burden to say, "Thanks for your love, but please go away," than to say, "I was hurting and no one cared for me." If someone says they need space, respect that. Otherwise, err on the side of presence.

Keep Remembering

One way you can be present for the long haul (even if you aren't in physical proximity) is to continue to remember the person long after their initial trauma is over. It's easy to move on with your life after the intensity of someone's trial has subsided, but those who don't forget are invaluable.

Pauline, a cancer survivor, said during her illness and treatments one of her neighbors periodically sent her cards. Her neighbor's quiet display of remembering meant so much to her. The neighbor continued sending cards for about a year!

Rita shared a conversation she had with a friend who lost his wife. Since they'd both experienced a similar plight, they were commiserating about how lonely it can be when people move on and you're still grieving. Then he told her about a certain couple who continued to send him handwritten letters well after most people had forgotten his sorrows and grief. Tears filled his eyes as he said, "They keep remembering."

After surviving cancer, author Michele Cushatt, who blogs at michelecushatt.com, wrote a post about grieving the life she once had. She says grieving people need others who will "commit to stick." She writes, "Affirm your love. Reassure your steadfast presence. It could take years and hundreds of the same questions and conversations. That's part of the process. Let them know you're not put off by it. Try something like, 'You can grieve as long as you need to. We can talk about this as much as necessary. You've earned it. And I'm not going anywhere.'"

The friend who loves their neighbor well in trial will continue to come alongside long after the initial hardship is over.

Chapter 8

love with food

Give us day by day our daily bread.
–Luke 11:3 NKJV

O ur family's happy place is at the lake in Northern Minnesota. We love to spend time together, and we love the privacy—rarely seeing anyone outside our family or invited friends when we're there. A visit to town to get groceries is a big adventure. Our primary goal is to rest in God's beautiful creation with those we love most.

We have briefly met several of our direct neighbors, but we aren't around enough to develop deep friendships. However a few summers ago, as we used the launch site on the lake for our boat, the launch owners mentioned that our neighbor two doors down had lost his wife to cancer over the winter while we were away.

For several days, I couldn't get him off my mind. I imagined him living alone now and grieving his wife of many decades. Finally, I determined to break out of my private cocoon and make an effort to be "neighborly." One of the best ways I know to do that? Deliver chicken noodle soup.

There was one big problem with my plan. I had barely spoken to this gentleman in our five years of being his lake neighbor. I think I had talked to him only twice, in passing. And now I was going to knock on his door and bring him soup? Oh, yeah, and tell him that someone else I barely know told me his wife had died?

Oh, dear. Sarah's best-laid plans. *Here we go again.*

Soup in hand, I waited until nearly 6 p.m. to make the long walk down his immaculate blacktop driveway. Maybe he wouldn't be home. Maybe I wouldn't have to face this awkward conversation. He'd never know I'd come. And I could just forget I'd ever had this foolish idea.

But when I rang the bell, not sure he'd even know who I was if he saw me, he answered the door. If he was surprised, he didn't show it. He made me feel as if we'd been friends forever.

"I made some soup and thought you might like some," I said.

I won't ever forget his response.

"I can't believe your timing. I just took a pre-packaged dinner out of the microwave and thought *this is inedible!* I'm diabetic, so I have to eat, and my wife used to take care of me that way. This meal has probably expired, and I couldn't eat it. And now here you are, bringing me homemade soup. I can't believe it! Thank you."

We proceeded to visit for the next half hour or so, and he slowly poured out the story of his wife's passing and all the sorrow he'd experienced over the last months. I never even had to tell him I already knew.

He seemed happy I stopped by. At the very least, he was thrilled about the edible dinner that would replace his freezer-burned microwave-dinner-for-one. As I made my way up the long, dark driveway, back to my peaceful retreat, I was reminded once again of a valuable lesson: food speaks a universal language of love.

When we don't know how to reach out in someone's time of need, food is a surefire way to start. And if we wonder if we should step out of our comfort zone to love and feed our neighbor, God usually answers our obedience with a resounding, YES!

Over the next several weeks that summer, I had the joy of sharing more treasures from my table with our sweet neighbor, along with many conversations in which he was able to give away a little bit of his grief to a welcome listener.

Top 10 Ingredients in the Recipe for Success

During my research, many folks chimed in with valuable advice regarding delivering meals. The consolidated opinions of many have come together to provide the meat of this chapter—ultimately helping you love your neighbor better through food. But before you head to the grocery store, let's take stock of a few basic do's and don'ts.

Do bring:
- ✓ Frozen meals for crock pot or oven
- ✓ Pantry meals-in-a-jar
- ✓ Cut up fruit and/or vegetables
- ✓ Sandwich fixings
- ✓ Pre-made, wrapped breakfast burritos
- ✓ "Anything with cheese" for families with kids (unless lactose-intolerant)
- ✓ Manageable or appropriate amounts
- ✓ Foods outside the normal ("Beef Tenderloin, yum!")
- ✓ Disposable pans, plates, containers, etc.

✓ Paper goods for no-mess clean up (napkins, plates, silverware, cups)
✓ Gift cards for groceries, deli, or take-out
✓ Healthy foods or options (for both kids and adults)
✓ Homemade treats as opposed to store bought

Don't bring:
✓ Only pasta based meals
✓ Anything too spicy (unless you know their tastes)
✓ Massive quantities (unless you know they're serving a crowd)
✓ Too many sweets (Multiple folks agreed on this!)
✓ Food containers that need returning
✓ Tons of pre-packaged store-bought foods.

Now let's dig in to the top 10 ingredients for successful delivery or preparation of meals.

1. Bring your "go-to" meal.
Bringing someone a meal doesn't have to be an occasion wrought with fear. Your abilities don't have to rival Martha Stewart, Rachael Ray, or Betty Crocker. My advice? Stick with a dish you're good at or make regularly. In other words, don't try to be gourmet. (Unless you are a chef, in which case, I'll send you my address.) Instead, do what you do best and "go-to" that meal or recipe when you find yourself needing to deliver someone a meal.

My best friend, Kay, who is prolific at loving her neighbor in trial, first taught me this valuable concept. I was preparing dinner to take to someone from my church one day when she said, "You're so lucky. You have a go–to meal."

Huh? I thought. Lucky that I was making chicken noodle soup and grilled ham and cheese for the thousandth time?

Precisely.

You see, I had my go–to, and I didn't even know it! From then on, I used that simple meal almost every time I cooked for a person or family in need.

Having a "go–to meal" isn't boring. It's *essential*. Admittedly, that's not what I thought whenever I wasted time pouring over *Bon Appétit* or searching Food Network.

> *Having a "go–to meal" isn't boring. It's* **essential**.

com for the perfect gourmet recipe. But if we're honest, we'll admit most of us can barely make it through the day with our own problems, family, job, chores, driving schedule, activities, and cooking. How can we add another family's dinner to the list?

By not putting on our Julia Child apron every time, that's how.

Keeping ingredients on hand for your specialty will take the guesswork—and the shopping—out of the equation. If the ingredients are in your cupboard or refrigerator, you are far more likely to act on those good intentions of helping someone instead of focusing on the reasons you can't. It becomes your go-to for a reason. And because your own family probably likes it too, you'll feed both your family and the one in need.

Not sure what recipe is your go-to? Ask your family to tell you their favorite meal you make. Or borrow a tried-and-true recipe from a friend. You can even borrow my go-to meals by downloading frequently requested favorites at www.sarahbeckman.org/resources.

But what if you don't even know how to turn on the oven? Then head to your favorite restaurant. Take-out can be a welcome guest in a home overflowing with lasagnas. Or try mixing a few store-bought items with homemade dishes to accentuate your areas of weakness. Many delis in fine grocery stores offer perfect alternatives if your cooking is less-than-stellar. As a guideline, stick with items you or your family have tried. Don't experiment on your friend with new, untested foods.

2. Coordinate your efforts.

Coordinating a meal calendar is the perfect way to pool resources and streamline the potential overflow of food. Angie told me that food can become overwhelming to someone in trial instead of being the blessing intended:

> Food makes people feel better to drop off but can be a huge pain for someone in crisis. It's best to get a calendar organized to coordinate meals better. A cooler on the step alleviates small talk the person may not be up for. People think they have to bring full meals, but I found cut up fruit, veggies or sandwich fixings to be more helpful.

For a list of food management sites see the Appendix or refer back to Chapter 3: In the Know.

3. Make extra.

After my neighbor Deborah's husband died, one of the simplest ways I loved her was by bringing her dinner. Because I was already cooking for my family of five, I could easily add enough for one person and share with her what I was already making. This removed the burden of making a full meal for her and allowed me to help more frequently.

If I made enchiladas, I would make a small pan of two and take it to her. If I made soup, she got her own helping. If I cooked a full meal, I made her a single portion plate to eat when she was ready. I also shared homemade baked goods. A half-dozen cookies or a slice or two of pie was a bright addition to a dark day.

If you're trying to serve an entire family, double what you're already making! Crock Pot meals multiply beautifully, often yielding much more than one family can eat.

With a dash of intentionality you can bestow blessing on someone in need—simply make a little extra and be willing to share what you have!

4. Be sensitive to their needs.

You don't want to unwittingly add stress to the person or family in need when you're bringing a meal. Follow their stated requests (if any) concerning diet, delivery time, allergies, or drop off location. It's important to think carefully about their situation and try your best to alleviate any unwelcome outcomes. Susie had this advice: "Meals are a blessing but raise several questions: Do I have to be home? Do I need to be presentable? Can you slip it in the doggy door? Is it rude to suggest that with four kids, we need to have something to feed them before 6:00?"

Susie's simple—even humorous—questions allow us to put ourselves in the place of the recipient. You have no idea how many visits there have been that day. You have no idea where the family stands emotionally at that moment. You have no idea just how many times they've been interrupted or if the patient or hurting friend is resting. You have no idea how many tears have been shed. You have no idea if they even have one more ounce of strength left to face one more human being at the door one more time this week. We should ask ourselves, "How can I make the meal and its delivery helpful, instead of harmful?"

Your biggest blessing is your silent service, without expectation of the "scoop," a thank you, or interaction.

5. Follow the guidelines.

Whenever possible, communicate with the recipient, or the meal coordinator, to be sure you're following the guidelines set forth by the

Don't assume you can be the exception to the rule, because other people will think they are too.

family. Don't assume you can be the exception to the rule, because other people will think they are too. And that adds up to lots of late deliveries, inconsistencies, and stressful meal times for a family/person who already has a plateful.

After my own experience (and at the urging of my wise husband), I always suggest that those receiving an extended period of meals leave a cooler outside the front door. This is an invaluable means of allowing the deliverer to leave the food without burdening the family receiving the meal.

Food delivery gets sticky when the well-meaning and kind person bringing said meal decides they want to see the grieving party, convalescing patient, or their relatives and talk to them about how things are going.

I said this was sticky.

You are making a kind gesture. You've taken time out of your life to shop, cook, prepare, deliver, and bless that sweet person or family with a meal, which is amazing! And necessary. However, depending on the situation, your innocent notion of wanting to ring the bell and deliver the food personally may just be the straw that breaks the camel's back, even if your motivation is pure or logistical (i.e. your meal needs to get in the oven)!

If you are a Tier 1 friend, you can likely ask permission to come in the house with the food, especially if there's another need involved or your presence is welcomed. If you are Tier 2, 3, or 4, you'd best drop that food in the cooler (if it's provided) or follow whatever rule they have established and make your merry way home. And please, know in your heart that you've been a bigger help than you realize simply because you followed the guidelines put in place for a reason.

6. Think "no returns."

Hot-dish containers. Soup Pots. Fancy Platters. A favorite 9 x 13 Pyrex pan. The brand new Tupperware you just purchased. Coolers. Whatever dish, container, or device you use to deliver a meal to someone in need, it is imperative you never expect to see it again.

If you've ever faced a life-altering loss or trial, you know lots of details fall through the cracks. Let me rephrase that—almost everything gets lost in the cracks. So please don't bring Aunt Florence's precious china serving dish to the mourning family across the street because, honestly, that's just plain inconsiderate.

Let me paint the picture.

For you, providing this meal is your only focus. You spend hours slaving over tater-tot hot dish. Looks matter as much as taste. You want to present it with flair and panache.

Something very different is going on inside the house where you're delivering the meal. No one is thinking clearly. They don't even feel like eating. But their friends and family keep telling them they should, so they swallow a few bites in between tears and call it a day. Sustenance is key for them, not presentation. And if you could see the huge pile of dishes to be returned already lining the back hall counter, the dining room table, and the kitchen counter, you'd understand.

Don't bring anything you need to see again in this lifetime.

Be prepared. Purchase a stash of disposable plastic ware of all sizes: the baking kind, the freezing kind, the small, big, colorful, or plain kind. This way you'll have what you might need on hand when called upon to deliver a meal. (For a great selection of disposable containers with style, check out www.simplybaked.us or www.maryandmartha.

com) Then the person you're trying to help doesn't have to think for a single minute about something as mundane as returning your dishes.

To be sure they know, include a note that says, "I hope you enjoy the meal, and rest assured I don't need any of my containers/dishes back."

7. Give gift cards.

Many friends have shared how valuable gift cards are in lieu of a prepared meal. Lora from California said, "I loved receiving a supermarket gift card during my own health struggles. So many other things require going out, returning dishes, or involve unhealthy foods. Gift cards are a gift anyone can give, even from afar, to let someone know they care without imposition or obligation."

Lora was also able to pay this blessing forward to help her friend with terminal brain cancer. "I sent my friend a gift card for a supermarket with a great deli near her. Before she passed away, she used it to special order a nice meal and have a romantic dinner at home with her husband without having to do all the work. It was a huge blessing for them!"

If you know the person well, you probably know where they like to shop or eat out. If not, enlist the advice of someone who knows them better or opt for another one of the suggestions I've given above.

8. Be specific.

If you're offering to bring a meal, pick a specific day or time instead of saying, "I can bring dinner." If your offer requires follow up from the individual/family you are serving, they may never respond. Which places both of you in an awkward position.

Remember to inquire about special dietary needs and try, whenever possible, to let the person know exactly what food you will bring. If you're able, ask them, "Would this type of food work for your family?" Your goal is to give them an opening to say whether or not they have an issue with what you're planning to bring without hurting your feelings. I also like to offer two options if I'm unsure about someone's tastes. This way they can choose without fear of offending.

9. Think long-term.

When a person has an acute need like surgery, death, or a health crisis, there is often an initial outpouring of food. However, people still need to feel a sense of connection and love after the chaos and distractions pass. That's when they are likely to begin feeling their grief, be even lonelier, or continue to struggle with physical limitations.

Bringing food in the months that follow critical times can be even more helpful than rushing over with a meal the moment you hear the news. It's important to continue to remember that the person might benefit from gifts of food long after the last hot dish has cooled.

10. Invite them to your house for a meal.

This option works well if you have a Tier 1 or 2 relationship with those enduring a crisis. If a family has experienced a death or has a prolonged illness in the house, invite them to your house for dinner. Sitting at the dinner table night after night with the glaring absence of a family member who has died or is hospitalized can take its toll on a family, as can eating strange food from plastic containers. An invitation to your home provides a needed distraction— and the added benefit for them of not having to clean up after the meal!

Invitations to visit your home are especially useful when men are the primary caregiver instead of the patient, but I would say most anyone would appreciate a break from cooking and cleaning up if you know them well enough to issue this invitation.

I hope this Top 10 List makes it easier for you to love your neighbor during their trial. With a little perseverance and planning, you'll be on your way to speaking the universal love language of food. And before you know it, you just might find yourself headed down the driveway of a stranger carrying a container of chicken noodle soup.

Chapter 9

do without asking

No act of kindness, no matter how small, is ever wasted.
–Aesop

We live in a society that relishes personal space. Privacy. Rules. Social courtesies. Yet one of the most common things I heard from people who've lived through really hard stuff is that some of the best help came from people who didn't ask permission first.

- ✓ A freshly mown lawn the day of the funeral.
- ✓ Trimmed bushes in the front yard the day of re-diagnosis.
- ✓ A batch of chocolate chip cookies delivered to the front door.
- ✓ A cleaning lady hired to ease the load.
- ✓ A circle of prayer in the yard the day of surgery.

Some of the best help came from people who didn't ask permission first.

Not asking permission to help someone is hard. We can feel awkward or worry our offering will be rejected in some way. But those who've lived through hardship remind us that there are so many decisions to make during crisis that they may not have time to get back to you. Sometimes asking is a bigger burden than the benefit of what you want to do for them.

Understand that I'm not talking about permission to handle personal issues or run someone's household. I am talking about tasks you know will need to be done anyway or those you would want done if you were in their situation. If you're worried about their response, should you act without their permission, ask yourself, "What harm can come if I _____?" (i.e. mow the grass, trim the bushes, plant the flowers, bring the meal, purchase some groceries, shovel the driveway, pray outside their house) If the answer is none, then you have the green light to go. If you're still unsure, ask yourself, "Would I feel blessed if someone did that for me?" If so, proceed.

If you do come up with a compelling reason not to do something, then don't. For example, you wouldn't want to pick up a person's child without their knowledge or get involved in personal family situations or decisions. When it comes to doing without asking, I believe with a little forethought you will know the line and when not to cross it.

For example, Jenny, a hospice nurse, remembers one patient's wife who spoke of a neighbor mowing their lawn while her husband was dying and then bringing them a bag of groceries without being asked. "Almost anyone can do that," she said.

Gary from Minnesota said he'd never forget the day a neighbor trimmed the shrubs without asking. He knew his significant other would have wanted that done, as she was very meticulous about her yard under normal circumstances. "When you're caring for someone in need, there are not enough hours in the day or room in the brain to process all the offers and get back to people," he said.

Alison from Georgia reminds us that "The 'call me if you want me to come and help' is useless. You appreciate someone who just shows up and does it. Most grieving people aren't aware enough at the time to call someone and say 'I need you to do this.' The people who served me most were those who didn't ask—they just did."

Small or large, spontaneous gestures were equally appreciated. Often people's first recollection was an instance where someone showed up unannounced and tended to a need they couldn't fill themselves or didn't have the wherewithal to recognize.

Kay said she will never forget looking out her window the day of her nephew's funeral to see our neighbor Deborah cutting the grass. She is still moved to tears every time she talks about it.

When I was put on bed rest because I went into pre-term labor, I wasn't sure how in the world we'd get through those months of me being unable to care for my two toddlers. There were countless acts of kindness, but the simplest still remain clear 14 years later.

A woman I had begun playing golf with the summer before showed up out of the blue to take care of my kids. I couldn't believe she would take time from her own hectic schedule, with two kids of her own, to offer a few hours of time to play with my toddlers. Had she asked to come, I probably would have said no because I would have felt like an imposition on her already busy days. When she showed up, heart and hands ready to serve, there was no way I could turn her away—because the fact of the matter was, I needed her.

David from New Mexico said some friends from church used their lunch break from work to pick up and deliver burgers to them in the hospital room where they sat with their child. He said, "They dropped off the food, gave us a hug, and went back to work." Different friends took David's car, filled it with gas, had the oil changed, topped off the fluids, and got it washed. He remembers, "Life was just too busy to do it ourselves at the time. " Both of those offerings impacted him enough that he still remembers, years later.

In an article titled "A New Normal: 10 Things I've Learned about Trauma," published on Sojourners.net, Catherine Woodiwiss gives insight into the nature of how people reach out to those experiencing trial: "If there are beatitudes for trauma, I'd say the first is, 'Blessed are those who give love to anyone in times of hurt, regardless of how recently they've talked or awkwardly reconnected or visited cross-country or ignored each other on the metro.' It may not look like what you'd request or expect, but there will be days when surprise love will be the sweetest."

The simple act of doing something you weren't asked to do is such a blessing.

If the garden glove fits, put it on and head over.

Chapter 10

listen well

Let every person be quick to hear, slow to speak, slow to anger.
–James 1:19b ESV

my friend Randy likes to say, "You can't learn anything new by talking." I think he heard it originally from his dad, but I'll give him the credit since he said it to me and it stuck.

I'm a talker by birthright. Whether it's my 100% Irish heritage or being the youngest of 14 children, I have an inherent need to talk loud enough and long enough to be heard. It's not my fault, it's in my genes!

That's why this chapter is harder for me than others in this book. But I'm trying to improve. In the corporate world, they call it a "Growth Edge." So because I like living on the edge, let's see if we can "grow" together.

Listening Has Value

One of my favorite movies is *Sleepless in Seattle*. It's the story of a widowed man who moves to Seattle with his eight-year-old son to start a new life after losing his wife to cancer. His son, Jonah, calls a radio show to get advice on how to help his grieving dad, Sam, find a new wife. After Jonah shares his heartbreaking story with the host, she encourages him to get his dad on the phone so she can talk to him. Then the therapist/radio host says this simple phrase: "Tell me about your wife."

Sam replies, "Well, how long is your show?"

This scene epitomizes how meaningful it is for someone to listen to a person after they've faced great loss or trial. Many people want to talk about the loss of a loved one but aren't always given opportunity. We fail to recognize the simple fact that listening is a valuable something we can do.

> *Listening is a valuable something we can do.*

The mother of a hospice patient shared these same sentiments. "After the death of my daughter, it was like people were afraid to say her name around me for fear of making me sad. I'm always thinking of her anyway and when someone says her name out loud, it makes me happy other people still think about her, too. I love to know she's not forgotten—that her life made a difference."

Rita from Minnesota agrees. "Life is divided into 'before' and 'after.' Remembering the person I loved is what I want to do."

We often rush to actions or words when someone is suffering (or do nothing for fear of doing the wrong thing). Instead, rush to be that welcome ear, listening when most others will not. Especially for those who are grieving. Pay attention to the signs if they don't want to talk, but don't be afraid of the tears that come with words.

It's been 18 years since I lost my brother, Dan, and I still welcome any occasion to talk about him. There are times those conversations bring me to tears, but I want to remember. The same principle applies to the many friends I have lost. I will see something that reminds me of my dear friends Deborah or Kelley, and even though I don't expect it, often the tears follow.

When people brush aside my tears or want to move away from the subject quickly, they devalue my grief. When you allow your friend to talk, even when it brings tears, you are among those who know how to effectively love others in their time of trial. Even if a person's trial isn't grief, the advice is the same: Listen. Listen. Listen.

Listen, Don't Fix

Susie is one of the funniest people I know. A mother of four, she and her family are living life to the fullest as missionaries in Rwanda even though she received a terminal brain cancer diagnosis four years ago. Just thinking about her sense of humor and her joy for life makes me smile. I am delighted and humbled by her and husband Ben's willing contributions to this book. I loved this advice from her regarding listening: "If I mention that I want a certain song played at my funeral, remember that. No need to make a big deal about it, just listen and take note. Oh, and maybe don't get so into it that you start giving me a playlist."

Like I said, she's hilarious!

Julia from Illinois said, "I think most of us want to 'fix' a loved one who is hurting. If I call to share my pain, please don't try to 'fix' me with what can only be considered a Band-Aid. Please listen and/or give me a hug instead."

If you've ever shared a struggle with someone and they immediately tried to fix it, you understand. This is especially true in dealing with the opposite sex. Women tend to be talkers. Men tend to be fixers. It's like when you've had a bad day. You want to vent to your husband and have him to listen attentively and validate your feelings, not sign you up for a self-help group just because you had a disagreement with your child's teacher.

> *Folks in trial don't necessarily want fixing, especially in "unfixable" situations.*

Similarly, folks in trial don't necessarily want fixing, especially in "unfixable" situations like illness or death. When you jump to "I can help you make this better," it frustrates them. They feel you're trivializing their troubles.

There is a time and a place for advice/suggestions, but if you want to stand out from the crowd and love your neighbor well in their trial, start by listening.

Listen, Don't Compare

When a person is in the middle of their own nightmare, they don't need to hear your story of your cousin's grandma's niece's fiancé who faced a similar diagnosis. (And didn't make it. Even worse!) Or how you lost someone you loved and still feel the pain. Or how your dog died so you know how they feel about losing their Mom. (Really?)

We've all experienced *that person,* who upon hearing bad news immediately embarks on their own harrowing tale. Before you know it, they've spent ten minutes talking about themselves, making your present situation a distant memory.

Please don't be *that person.* There is a time and place for sharing a relevant trial, but as a rule, err on the side of more listening and less talking about yourself. (Remember: It's not about you!)

When someone is grieving a loved one, stick to listening and focus on her loss. Julia cautions against this phenomenon I call "comparative grief":

One thing that isn't helpful is the well-meaning friend who tries to empathize by letting you know they went through something similar. "I know how you feel because I also experienced X loss." Sometimes this turns into a grief comparison. I think of some of the trials I've seen friends go through: giving birth to a stillborn child, seven miscarriages, not being able to have a child then adopting only to have the adoption reversed two years later, having your only child leave for college. All of these women have experienced the loss of a child. Is one greater, worse, or less painful than another? Do not compare or relate your grief to a friend's. We have all experienced pain, but each grief is different.

Claire, a 14-year-old from Minnesota, spoke of her grief after losing her older brother years earlier. In her youthful candor and wisdom, she said, "I hated when people said, 'I know how you feel.' I wanted to kill them. Even if they really had lost a brother, it wasn't *my* brother. I hated them 'smooshing in' on my grief with their own."

If the trial is something like divorce, shared illness, or caring for aging parents, and you both have that experience in common, there may be opportunity for you to share your insights when the time is right. But use caution and prayer as your guide, and only share if your input is welcomed and/or relevant. For more guidance on this topic see Chapter 22: When You've Been There.

Ask Questions

One way to be sure you have ample opportunity to listen is to ask questions. If you're a talker like me, this can be a great tool. You get to talk—but only in questions. You can ask how they feel about the person they are grieving if there has been a death or about the "life" they're grieving in the case of illness or divorce.

On the other hand, do be cautious to allow lots of normal conversation and activity, too. A tool that is helpful in this case is using open-ended questions as opposed to close-ended questions.

Open-ended questions start with words like how, why, what, tell me about, and describe. They cannot be answered with one word but require explanation or conversation. If you focus on open-ended questions, you will be on your way to meaningful dialogue instead of simple answers to questions. (Hint: This tool is helpful in any area of your life, especially if you have teenagers!) If you practice becoming a better listener in everyday situations, you will be better prepared for success when someone you care about is facing trial.

One friend said she welcomed any excuse to talk about her son after he died but said people didn't ask about him for fear it would make her sad. She recommends offering an opportunity for the person to "go there"—all the while watching for signs they don't want to discuss their situation.

If you ask an open-ended question and they open the door on hard topics, then walk in with a tender, listening heart. If they close the door, don't push but continue to be available. Chances are that if you've offered to listen once and they shut you down, they may come back to you when they are ready to talk.

Simply put, when someone you care about is facing trial, your job is to be quiet and listen. Now that's not so hard, is it?

Chapter 11

give good gifts

For God loves a cheerful giver.
–2 Corinthians 9:7b NIV

Saying you're writing a book is a great conversation starter. One day the subject came up with my hair stylist, Madi. She was really intrigued by a book that would give people ideas how to help someone in a tough spot. She admitted that her fear of rejection, interfering, or making things worse often kept her from reaching out to someone in need. But she also said she usually really wants to help.

Bingo! People like her are the reason I wrote this book.

Amazing the amount of research you can get done with foils in your hair and sporting a sweaty black cape. We didn't stop talking the entire two hours I sat in her chair, and she had far more valuable insights than she realized.

She opened up about family, friends, and troubles they'd been through. And despite her fears, there were plenty of instances when she had done just the right thing! In fact, she put into words one of my new favorite ways to choose gifts. It's low investment and high return, which is always a winning combination.

Find Their Favorites

Madi's simple principle translates into an amazing way to give a thoughtful, out of the ordinary gift. Simply, find a favorite item your friend in need likes and bring it to them!

> *Find a favorite item your friend in need likes and bring it to them!*

Madi's friend was going through a hard time, and his favorite vices were Reese's Peanut Butter Cups and Red Bull. As a result, she tried to keep Red Bull and Reese's on hand, so whenever she saw him she could give them to him. She even stopped by his work to deliver them on occasion, bringing a smile to his face.

Simple, thoughtful, and effective.

Because when the going is rough, sometimes you just need Reese's and Red Bull.

After she shared her story, I remembered a similar experience. One of my dear friends is a fresh fruit fanatic. He doesn't like to have junk food around, and even though friends tease him about it, it's important to him to eat healthy. But grocery shopping isn't always on the top of the list when your life is in crisis.

While his wife was sick, he faced many challenges balancing work, children, and hospital visits. Knowing I might see him at the hospital one day, I brought a tray of raspberries with me. We met in the hallway as he was heading home. I handed him the unadorned plastic container filled with bright red fruit. He looked surprised, but in the span of our five-minute conversation, he polished off the entire container of fruit while standing in the hospital corridor. It wasn't anything fancy; it was a simple way to show I cared, even though I felt helpless to change his difficult reality.

Because when the going is rough, sometimes you just need an entire package of raspberries.

When my close friend Deborah was dying of cancer, she requested a favor of me. How could I deny a dying woman's request? Yet I was unsure of what she might ask—afraid of the ramifications. She told me how much her sweet and cherished boyfriend, Gary, loved Jelly Bellies. And then she asked, "Could you please get him some from time to time?"

The next time I was at the store, I picked up a bag of those precious little gems and took them to the house. When Gary saw them, he knew it was her idea because I never would have known his penchant for that candy. Despite her limited physical ability at the time, she made an effort to do something nice for him, and it touched him in a profound way. This was such an easy way to help my friend show her loved one how special he was to her that it bears repeating to you.

Because when the going is rough, sometimes you just need a bag of Jelly Bellies.

If you want to bless someone in trial on a level beyond the perfunctory, "bring a meal or send a card option," gifting favorites will serve you well. Find their favorites. Remember their favorites. And take time to deliver them. Minimum effort. Maximum return.

The important thing is to customize your offering based on who they are and what they like. To get your creative juices flowing, you can start by asking a few questions:

✓ Do they love a certain food?

✓ Do they like certain music?

✓ Is there a recipe their kids loved that you've made?

✓ Do they have a favorite restaurant you could order take out from?

✓ Is there a tradition you can help them maintain or continue?

✓ Do they love kids? Can your kids bring some youthful joy?

✓ Do they like certain types of movies?

✓ Do they have an affinity for any special sport/holiday/event?

There are times we will have no words. It's those times gifting a "favorite" says what we cannot.

Good Gift Suggestions

I love giving gifts! I thrill at the prospect of giving a well-chosen, unique gift. Just ask my family. I can hardly wait until a gift-giving occasion and have been known to give gifts early out of pure impatience. I like giving gifts as much, if not more, than receiving them.

I've been around enough hospital rooms and sick beds—including my own—to know that you can only have so many inspirational books or trinkets for your nightstand table. And so this chapter is full of insights from friends who've walked the rough waters of trial and want you to know exactly what kinds of gifts will be well received. Get your highlighters out. Great gifts, here we come!

Kris from Minnesota, a breast cancer survivor, shares her list of go-to gifts for friends in crisis.

✓ Massage coupons

✓ Manicure/pedicure certificates

✓ Comfy socks with no-slip bottoms (Kris suggests Karen Neuburger/Smartwool.)

✓ Pajamas or comfortable tops and bottoms (Karen Neuburger is a good option.)
✓ Front-opening shirts and jackets (especially for breast cancer patients)
✓ Magna Doodle if patient is unable to speak (mouth or tongue surgery or tracheotomy)
✓ Scarves and/or hats for chemotherapy patients

These treasures are a far cry from the standard dust-collecting items we often gift in times of crisis. Susie has good recommendations, too:

Fun, random gifts are great. A cute pair of earrings, a book you loved (that isn't about cancer or death). Someone dropped a box off at my door with a tag that said, "Thought you could use a little sunshine!" It was full of random yellow stuff from the dollar store. Loved it! Someone else gave me a very generous gift certificate to an expensive salon that allowed me to go *by myself* and get my hair done *when I was ready*. I didn't feel obligated to bring this person along or get her advice on my hair.

My pals Pauline, Angie, and Karen all recommend giving a "blessings journal" as a great way to help a friend focus on the good instead of the bad in their circumstance. Angie was on the receiving end of this gift, too. When a friend suggested Angie start a journal and write down at least one blessing a day, Angie said, "It was the single best advice anyone gave me."

Although she admits such a gift is counter-intuitive to what you'd expect from someone when you're in the middle of a dire circumstance, it proved very therapeutic for her. Now whenever Angie hears of someone who has received a cancer or Type I diabetes diagnosis, she puts together a care package with a small journal and note telling them to look for one blessing a day, write it down, and put their focus there.

Angie loves to gift a particular journal she's found at Barnes and Noble. It comes with a Bible verse on the cover—Jeremiah 29:11: "For I know the plans I have for you, declares the Lord, plans to prosper you and not to harm you, plans to give you a hope and future." It also has Scripture and other inspirational quotes on the bottom of the blank pages.

Even if someone isn't a writer, journaling can be very helpful. Or they can use the blank book to list gifts, visits, phone calls, to-dos, or meaningful events throughout their trial. I personally love a brand spanking-new notebook, trial or not!

When Martha from Pennsylvania lost her brother, she appreciated tender, practical and even "trivial" gifts:

> A couple of generous friends put together the most thoughtful grieving-oriented care package full of miscellaneous items: tissues, waterproof mascara, hand sanitizer, immunity-boosting vitamins/essential oils, worship CDs, tons of healthy (and some not-as-healthy) snacks/treats, hydrating beverages (coconut water), blank notecards/stamps, Starbucks gift cards, index cards filled with passages of Scripture, etc. This heartfelt gift blessed me while meeting a lot of practical needs!

Martha also appreciated "the gift of pampering." This gift will translate in different ways to different individuals: a gift card for a massage or pedicure, a weekend away, childcare, etc. She said, "When you are feeling so worn down after—or in the midst of—a season of grief, something to pamper yourself (even if it seems superficial) can really refresh your spirit!"

During Susie's time of need, gift cards equaled freedom. "I could get myself what I needed when I needed it without having to question the cost." Susie's husband was the primary gift card user because she was the "patient." She believes gift cards are also a great option for long-term helpers, like parents or other family, so they don't feel obligated to pay for every meal out when caregiving. When she regained her strength, she also used gift cards for lunch with friends when she started to get stir crazy in her house.

You can also mine the following lists for specific ideas based on gender and/or age category. And consider absolving the person of a thank you note by cleverly making that part of your gift. To do this, include a note saying, "Part of my gift to you is that I don't want or expect a thank you. I am delighted to help and trust that you have plenty on your plate without adding thanking me to it." (This goes for any gift of time, service, food, or tangible gifts!)

> *Consider absolving the person of a thank you note by cleverly making that part of your gift.*

Gifts for women:
- ✓ Salon gift cards, especially when a friend might be losing part or all of her hair from effects of chemotherapy
- ✓ Massage gift cards
- ✓ Pedicure/Manicure gift cards
- ✓ Blooming indoor flower basket or outdoor flowering pots
- ✓ Green plants (hearty ones that are easy to keep alive)
- ✓ Grocery gift cards
- ✓ Faith-based gifts (see separate list)
- ✓ Gas cards

- ✓ Take-out restaurant gift card
- ✓ Prayer shawl
- ✓ Cozy throw blanket
- ✓ Lumbar pillow
- ✓ Pajamas
- ✓ Sunglasses
- ✓ Under eye cold packs (or hot or herbal varieties)
- ✓ Essential oils (be careful not to undermine/discredit current treatments)
- ✓ House cleaning (1x or ongoing)
- ✓ Night on the town (tickets to a show/event, dinner gift card, babysitting)
- ✓ Books

Gifts for men:
- ✓ Books (action/adventure series)
- ✓ Movies sets (such as *Star Wars*, *Lord of the Rings*, *The Godfather*)
- ✓ Magazines
- ✓ Favorite food, candy, beverage
- ✓ Blanket
- ✓ Music
- ✓ Tickets to sporting event or concert
- ✓ Small remote-control helicopter (www.amazon.com)
- ✓ TV Series sets
- ✓ Car care (oil change, wash/vacuum)
- ✓ Lawn care/yard maintenance
- ✓ Snow or leaf removal
- ✓ Childcare
- ✓ Night out with the guys
- ✓ Pajama pants or comfortable loungewear (in the case of illness)

Gifts for teens:
- ✓ Movies
- ✓ Books
- ✓ Music
- ✓ iTunes gift card
- ✓ Amazon gift card
- ✓ Netflix subscription
- ✓ Sketch book, pencils/pens
- ✓ Journal
- ✓ Pajamas/slippers/socks
- ✓ Small pillow/throw blanket
- ✓ Candy/gum/snacks
- ✓ Games (Chess, Backgammon, Settler's of Catan, Rummikub, Catch Phrase, etc)
- ✓ Playing cards
- ✓ Coffee, tea, or juice gift cards (Starbucks, Boba Tea, Jamba Juice, Orange Julius)
- ✓ Frozen yogurt/ice cream gift cards
- ✓ Fast food gift cards
- ✓ Movie gift cards (Fandango = any theater)
- ✓ Faith/Inspirational gift
- ✓ Scarves/Hats
- ✓ Music player and/or small speaker
- ✓ Favorite food, candy, beverage

Gifts for young children:
- ✓ DVDs
- ✓ Coloring books with crayons/markers
- ✓ Books
- ✓ Games—travel-sized if hospitalized (Blokus, Rummikub, Uno, Bananagrams, etc.)

✓ iTunes gift card
✓ LEGOS (boys)
✓ My Little Pony/Littlest Pet Shop (girls)
✓ Pillow Pets
✓ Card games
✓ Favorite food, candy, beverage

Faith/inspirational gifts:

There are many options for faith-based gifts. You can head to your local church bookstore, Christian bookstore or online Christian gift outlet (www.cbd.com, www.dayspring.com) to choose a gift right for the situation. The important thing is to help the person in trial put their focus on things above, not necessarily on their present circumstance.

Suggestions include:

✓ Plaque
✓ Framed Scripture
✓ Cross
✓ Jewelry
✓ Scripture cards
✓ Devotional
✓ Books
✓ Bible study
✓ Christian concert tickets
✓ Christian conference tickets

Gift cards for any age/gender:

✓ Restaurants
✓ Coffee
✓ Clothing

- ✓ Groceries
- ✓ Gas
- ✓ Spa
- ✓ Salon
- ✓ Christian book store
- ✓ Amazon
- ✓ Visa, Master Card, or American Express

Homemade/DIY gifts on a budget:

The following can go into small mason jars (see www.pinterest.com):

- ✓ Homemade sugar scrub
- ✓ Homemade granola
- ✓ Fizzy peppermint bath salts
- ✓ Lavender body butter
- ✓ Blessings jar

Other DIY gift ideas:

- ✓ Prayer box using empty breath mint tins
- ✓ Fleece tie pillow or blanket
- ✓ Personalized scripture cards (www.sarahbeckman.org/printable-scripture-cards)

Customized gift baskets

Create a custom gift basket by combining any gender/age appropriate item(s) from the above lists with any of the following:

- ✓ Magazines (Can be from your own collection, light reading topics that aren't associated with their trial)
- ✓ Thank you notes or blank notecards with stamps

✓ Paper goods, plastic ware, disposable cups
✓ Coffee or tea (Starbuck's VIA instant coffee if they're hospitalized and want good coffee)
✓ Blessings journal
✓ Devotional book (See Resources in Appendix for specific title ideas)
✓ Inspirational or faith-based gift
✓ Fuzzy socks
✓ Sparkling water or fresh juices
✓ Your favorite movie or book (but please, not your own copy if you want it back)
✓ Kleenex-to-go packs
✓ Sudafed (relieves crying induced headaches) and Tums
✓ Gum or mints
✓ Hand sanitizer
✓ Hand lotion
✓ Small toy or treats for pets

Consumable gift baskets

If the person you are helping is part of a large network of support, too much "stuff" can easily overwhelm while the necessities get lost. If you are grieving a loved one or have received a difficult diagnosis, the last thing you're thinking is "do we have enough toilet paper in the house?" Consider giving practical items with a note that says something like, "Here are a few staples in case you don't have time to get to the store."

Consumable household gift baskets might include:

✓ Household items (tissues, paper towels, toilet paper, garbage bags)
✓ Disposable plates, cups, napkins, silverware
✓ Decorative plates and napkins

- ✓ Hand soap, dish detergent, lotion
- ✓ New kitchen towels/wash cloths/sponges
- ✓ Bottled juices, soft drinks, water, teas
- ✓ Ground coffee/creamer/to-go cups
- ✓ Snacks (chips, cookies, pretzels, granola, trail mix)

Gifts are a welcome blessing when they are thoughtful and appropriate. Here's to giving good gifts in your future!

Chapter 12

choose wise words

Death and life are in the power of the tongue.
–Proverbs 18:21 ESV

P ain is a strong memory maker. Cutting words and insensitive platitudes are more often remembered than the positive actions of people who help. Our words can even wound unintentionally. Many friends still bristle as they share stories of painful remarks or hurtful emails from friends or family.

In a time of trial, we want nothing more than to say something comforting and helpful to someone we care about, so why are we determined to say something even when we know our words could hurt? Human nature makes it hard to keep our mouths shut. We've been wired to try to say the perfect thing, but we can end up hurting when we intend to heal.

You've read chapters about the importance of simply being present and of listening; however there will be times you need to use words. That's why this chapter is critical. As you strive to speak encouraging words, start with these guidelines in mind.

Less Is More

Remember Job's friends from the Bible? They were the ones who showed up to comfort and sympathize with their friend. "Then they sat on the ground with him for seven days and seven nights. No one said a word to him, because they saw how great his suffering was." (Job 2:13 NIV)

No one said a word.

For seven days and nights.

That might sound extreme, but there's a reason the phrase "silence is golden" was coined.

The truth is, nothing we say can take away someone else's pain in the moment.

The truth is, nothing we say can take away someone else's pain in the moment.

My advice to you is to keep it simple. We worry that "Sorry for your loss" is trite or common, but wouldn't you rather be common instead of hurtful? When in doubt, more listening and less talking is always a good idea. Of course there will be times to speak, especially if you have a long-term, close relationship (Tier 1) with someone who's hurting, but more often than not, less is best, especially in the case of death or newly diagnosed health concerns.

Jenny, a hospice nurse, reminds us of this. "Over the years, I've tried so hard to say the right thing at the right time to my patients or their families in order to ease the pain of loss and grief. Sometimes my words have helped. Other times I royally messed up and should've kept my mouth shut. Silence would've been more helpful than the rambling words I tried to mutter."

Acknowledge, Affirm, Express (AAE)

Consider using my AAE formula if you need further guidance on what to say, or your foot has gotten your mouth into trouble before.

A) Acknowledge their situation.

Acknowledging their situation means saying something like, "I'm sorry that you are facing _____." Remember to keep this statement about them. (It's not about you!) The important part is to validate their situation, not fix it, as we learned in Chapter 10: Listen Well. Let them know you care, but stop short of analyzing or explaining things away.

A) Affirm their feelings.

Affirming their feelings would look something like "I can see how you would feel that way." But be careful not to put feelings they haven't stated into their mouth. If they've expressed their feelings, you can restate what they told you, but don't project your own feelings onto them.

For example, if they say they are depressed, disappointed, angry, unclear, or any other emotion, you can affirm their feelings by saying, "Yes, you have every right to feel that way!" instead of coming at them first with "This must be so devastating/frustrating/damaging/maddening/relieving/horrifying/ disheartening for you."

Give them permission to feel the way they're feeling. We should never expect someone to respond in the way we might, so let each person deal with their trial in their own way. Don't push them to move through or move on immediately. They need your encouragement to take all the time they need. And bear in mind, in many situations, life will never be the same again.

E) Express your empathy.

Expressing your empathy could sound like, "I am with you, I'll be here for you, I'm standing beside you in this hard thing." Another way to express empathy to someone grieving is by talking about the person they lost, saying what you will miss about them or what you loved about their personality or life.

Remember, we learned that specific offers are more helpful and more likely to be accepted, so you might want to skip the "Let me know what I can do" phrase.

As you will learn in the remainder of this chapter, there are other ways to be effective without saying too much. And there are words to watch out for, too.

Use Encouraging Scripture

God's word is living and active. I know no better tool to bring hope and wisdom in the darkness, when human ability is limited. The Appendix of this book has a resource guide of Scriptures by topic that you may want to use to begin. I've also included a link to an online resource of printable Scripture cards you can customize by inserting the person's name into specific verses. These have proven invaluable to many people I know in times of trial and would be a great way to express your love.

Similarly, Angie recommends compiling a "cheat sheet" of Bible verses focused on encouragement to use in cards, Caring Bridge entries, etc. Having easy access to those verses will help when you don't know what to write or say. Choose verses that will help the person facing trial to remain focused on God in their darkest hour.

Offer to Pray

When words don't come easily and you're worried about saying the right or wrong thing, a great solution is to ask the person how you might pray for them. The question, "How can I be praying for you?" allows the person to talk about what they want or need as opposed to you guessing or saying the wrong thing by putting forth your agenda.

In times of great trial, prayer can be a salve to someone's wounds. If you offer to pray, either right then or later on your own, you will reach into their life with the power of words lifted before God on their behalf. We cover this more in depth in Chapter 16: Pray Diligently.

Focus on the Person, Not the Situation

Especially in the case of death, one valuable way to express your sympathy is to talk about the person who died—what they meant to you, meaningful memories about them, or attributes of their personality and life that stood out to you.

A friend of mine recently lost her husband to a sudden heart attack. When she shared the news on her Facebook page, she included this statement: "We're asking for memories and anecdotes or ways that {he} touched your life in lieu of condolences."

I love this idea! It is so meaningful to have people talk about the loved one who has died. Those grieving want to focus on the person, not the loss. And if you've ever lost someone you love, you understand how special those sentiments are in lieu of empty words that can be forgotten.

If you know someone who has recently been diagnosed with a life-altering illness or disease, you also want to focus on the person, not the illness. If you can encourage them with words about their courage, strength, fortitude, or attitude, you place emphasis on the person, not their condition. Talking about who they are, instead of what ailment they have, helps forge hope and a positive countenance for them too.

Vent Appropriately

When someone you care about is facing trial, you will no doubt experience many of your own challenging feelings or emotions. You might be grieving, afraid, distressed, sad, worried, frustrated, or overwhelmed in your own right. This can be a lot to bear, and could cause you to express your emotions to the wrong person, or in the wrong way.

When my sister's husband was facing terminal Melanoma, she had many challenging emotions and feelings even though she wasn't the direct patient. I remember advising her to share her struggles with those of us who weren't as directly affected by Tom's illness. By venting to her family or friends, instead of Tom, she was able to express her own feelings and emotions without adding her burden to his.

Since that time, I discovered this concept succinctly stated in an online article from the LA Times titled "How Not to Say the Wrong Thing." Author Susan Silk presents what she calls the Silk Ring Theory, which is summarized by the concept of "Comfort In, Dump Out." This statement speaks a real truth about how we can express our own feelings and to whom it's appropriate to do so.

If you envision a dartboard with concentric circles, the patient is in the bull's-eye. Their family and those people closest to them are in the next outer circle (Tier 1), and the circles of affinity to the person continue moving outward with the furthest circle from the bull's-eye being those who know the person least (Tier 4).

Silk contends that we should always provide comfort to those in the circle smaller than ours (inward) and we should only "dump" our emotions, feelings, heartbreaks, or struggles into the circles larger than ours (outward). She writes, "If you want to scream or cry or complain, if you want to tell someone how shocked you are or how icky you feel, or whine about how it reminds you of all the terrible things that have happened to you lately, that's fine. It's a perfectly normal response. Just do it to someone in a bigger ring."

This is a powerful reminder of where to put those very real feelings . . . and where not to.

Words to Avoid

So far we've talked about what to say, but what not to say might be even more important. Here are some ways you can avoid wounding with your words when you come alongside those experiencing a significant trial.

Avoid "true but not helpful" statements.

My good friend Keith Ferrin says, "Just because it's true, doesn't make it helpful." Truer words have never been spoken.

So many things we could choose to say in someone's time of trial are true, but often it's not helpful to say them. For example, when a mom has just lost her infant child, she doesn't necessarily want to hear her child is "in a better place," even if it is true. She wants her baby to be in this place, in this moment with her. Unwittingly, we've just made her feel worse because we are insensitive to her new reality.

There are so many examples of "true but not helpful" phrases. To increase my sampling, I took a Facebook poll. The responses rolled in. It seems many folks have been wounded by such phrases.

Here is a sampling:

- "They're in a better place."
- "Their suffering is over."
- "Heaven needed them more than you."
- "At least you have other kids."
- "At least you have one healthy baby."
- "At least you didn't lose everything."
- "You're better off without him/her."
- "Why do you care? He was never that good to you."
- "It must have been their time."
- "It must have been God's will."
- "God will work all things for good. You'll see."

- "At least it was quick and she didn't suffer from a long illness like cancer."
- "God must have been finished with him."
- "God will bring someone else into your life to offset the pain."
- "Time heals all wounds."
- "It's for the best."
- "You're so lucky you're young enough to have more children."
- "At least it {miscarriage} happened now instead of later on, when it would have been even worse."
- "Just be thankful he/she's out of your life."
- "You really dodged a bullet there."

It's important to clarify that all of these statements are essentially *true* (especially the many spoken in a vernacular of faith), but people weren't comforted or helped by them. And I'm guessing if you're like me, you've probably said one or two of these yourself. (Insert groan.)

Becky from Missouri describes unhelpful phrases like these as "trying to look for the 'silver lining' in other people's grief, finding ways to diminish their loss, or trying to get people to move past the sadness faster than they're ready to."

Of course the words we've been talking about are not to be mistaken with the horrifying things people say that aren't helpful *or* true. For example, "Surely you did something to deserve this." Or "They got what was coming to them."

I'm sure there are countless other phrases I could mention here, but let's distill it down to this: Think you before you speak.

Listen more and speak less, and you'll be heading in the right direction.

Avoid platitudes.

In tough situations, people often turn to platitudes. Platitudes can be defined as banal, trite, or stale remarks. These rote phrases are often used when we don't know what to say. Some of them fall into our "true but not helpful" category; others might be true, false or just common. But if you heed the advice given above—less is more—and skip the platitudes, you will be leaps and bounds ahead of those who don't. Remember, it's likely they've heard these phrases countless times, and they just get tired of hearing them.

The movie *St. Vincent* is about a grumpy, drunken army veteran named Vincent who is befriended by a young boy who moves in next door. After Vincent lost his wife to Alzheimer's disease, he is sitting alone outside his house with her ashes in a box next to him.

The boy comes over and says, "Sorry, Vin, for your loss."

Vincent replies, "Never understood why people say that."

The boy answers, "They don't know what else to say."

"How about 'What was she like? Do you miss her? What are you going to do now?'"

"Sorry for your loss" is an easy thing to say when you're not sure what else to say. I wouldn't classify it as harmful, but if the occasion arises, do think outside the box and try some of the other suggestions from this and other chapters.

Julia from Illinois remembers when she was grieving her dad. Her mom, who was grieving too, shared platitudes with her, thinking they would bring comfort. Julia told her mom, "Using logic to cure an emotional pain just doesn't work. The heart has to heal from the inside out—with love, not logic."

Avoid putting words in their mouth.

We often overstep our bounds by trying to help our loved ones see things through rose-colored-glasses. It's important to allow them to journey through their hardship in their own way. In her article on sojourners.net, Catherine Woodiwiss recommends allowing people to discover for themselves where they are, not deciding for them:

> Someone who has suffered trauma may say, "This made me stronger," or "I'm lucky it's only (x) and not (z)." That is their prerogative. There is an enormous gulf between having someone else thrust his unsolicited or misapplied silver linings onto you and discovering hope for one's self. . . . Give the person struggling through trauma the dignity of discovering and owning for himself where, and if, hope endures.

Using AAE as a means to express your care would be a great way to affirm the feelings of the person you're reaching out to as opposed to inserting your perspective on their situation. They need to feel how they're feeling, not how you think or want them to feel. Many people tire of other's opinions about how they should be handling their reality.

Avoid medical or treatment advice.
Many well-intentioned folks have done more harm than good by recommending every treatment option they've ever heard of in the name of being helpful. If your friend/family/loved one has a health related trial (cancer, illness, ongoing condition), they are likely under the care of professionals.

Rule of thumb: *If they don't ask your advice, don't give it.*

During my years of debilitating back issues, I was under the care of both a chiropractor and medical doctor. I can't tell you how many suggestions I received of how to "fix" my condition. Pilates, physical therapy, acupuncture, artificial disk replacement, core strengthening, inversion machines, epidurals. You name it, people recommended it.

The advice was given with a sincere desire to help. But over time, it wore me out. Honestly, more than one person unwittingly made me feel like I had done something to deserve my back issues. But my back pain is genetic. Along with over half of my 13 siblings, I have degenerative disk disease. I was born with it. Yes, there are things I can do to help myself, but after trying many treatments, surgery was my best option. Yet every time I said I was having surgery, someone new would tell me of a surefire cure I had to try!

My back issues were a big deal to me, but they don't compare to other, more severe and long-term diseases like MS, cancer, Alzheimer's, Lou Gehrig's, Parkinson's, fibromyalgia, or countless others. And I know many folks facing those health concerns who agree: Don't give unending medical advice unless I ask for it.

So please don't overwhelm your friends with constant suggestions of how they can treat their ailment. This makes them feel like it's their fault they are ill (most diseases are indiscriminate), and it undermines the therapy or treatment the person has chosen.

Susie from Rwanda says,

> This is tricky, because some advice is helpful, and I know it's all well meant. But it's just too hard to sort through. My husband was my dumping ground for advice. Whenever someone had a book or article I had to read or a doctor I had to check out or a diet I had to try, my standard answer was, "I don't have the capacity to think about that right now. Can you email my husband and he'll take a look at it?"

If you have expertise in an area, offer to be the gatekeeper who deals with all the health suggestions for your friend/loved one. Then the one in the health crisis has a place to refer those folks with advice so they feel heard and valued for their offers of help. You can wade through the suggestions on behalf of your friend to see what has merit if they are looking for advice or ideas pertaining to their situation.

Avoid sharing horror stories.

When people's lives are turned upside down by trial, you don't need to increase their stress or pain by regaling them with the worst story you've ever heard that pertains to

> *Just because it's true doesn't make it helpful.*

your situation. Remember, "just because it's true doesn't make it helpful."

In her book *Undone: A Story of Making Peace with an Unexpected Life*, author Michele Cushatt writes of people who felt the need to share their less-than-desirable situations with her when they learned of her cancer diagnosis:

"My brother was just diagnosed with Stage 4 liver cancer. They don't think he's going to make it."

"My friend was diagnosed with the same kind of cancer as you. He died a few months ago."

"My mom was cancer-free for years. Then it came back. It was awful."

If you've ever faced loss or a life-changing diagnosis, I'm guessing you've got tales of your own. When we hear of someone's trial, our first inclination is often to relate to them through our own experience or knowledge. This can be a valuable tool. However, what inadvertently happens is that you take the focus off them (which is where it needs to be) and put it on yourself when you relate your trial (or that of your grandma's friend's sister).

Adrienne from Colorado said it this way: "Any comment that makes my grief about the person who is making the comment is unhelpful in a time of trial."

You get my point. Don't regale your friend with your personal experience or your "friend of a friend" story. Focus on their situation and how you can best serve and empathize with them.

Most importantly, stay positive. Think about what you say before you say it. And don't share insanely terrible outcomes with someone when your intention is to bring help or hope.

Guard your tongue. It can either bring life or pain. You get to choose.

Choose wisely.

Chapter 13

think outside the box

Try to be a rainbow in someone's cloud.
–Maya Angelou

W hen my kids were little, we hired an amazing woman to babysit them a few times a week so I could volunteer, do errands, go to Bible study, or just get a break for a few hours. Jackie was like a family member and treated my kids as her own. She did laundry, tidied the house, crafted with the kids, snuggled with them, and loved on them. Our whole family adored her.

While I was on bed rest, she often put in extra hours for us when my husband, Craig, had to travel. No wage could compensate her sufficiently for all she did for our family, but what I did pay quickly added up during those months.

I will never forget when she offered to stay in the evening beyond her normal hours—for free—so Craig could have some time away from the house to get a break from carrying all the extra weight in our family's trial. And she didn't do it just once. She did it once a week until my daughter was born!

This gift was something I never recognized Craig needed because I was so overwhelmed creating a care plan for our family and coordinating schedules. Managing my health and our growing family from flat in my bed was all I could handle. I was tapped out.

She, on the other hand, saw the reality: Craig was working every day, coming home and making meals (even if they were provided he still had to serve everyone), cleaning up, putting two kids to bed, and taking care of me. He had not one ounce of down time for himself. Her gift was so precious because she looked beyond me and saw the other people in my life who were also struggling.

> *It's important to look for the collateral damage that is caused by the storm of someone's trial.*

It's important to look for the collateral damage that is caused by the storm of someone's trial. Thank you, Jackie, for teaching me that all those years ago.

Look Beyond

Many times when a person is sick or faced with a life-altering situation, we think of only the affected person. In the case of a death, we think of the immediate family. These thoughts are critical, but there are other ways to be useful as it relates to the ancillary people involved. If you think of the other possibilities, such as the care-giving spouse, extended family, close friends, children, older relatives that may be living in the home, or even family pets that need care, you can tap a niche that isn't always addressed.

If you are Tier 2, 3, or 4, this would be a wonderful way for you to be a resource to those secondarily affected parties—which is often as necessary as helping the primary person in need.

Spouse

When a married person has a long-term illness or challenging diagnosis, the affected party receives the majority of the support. While this is vastly important, it is a special person who looks beyond the "patient" to see the spouse who is hurting just as much and has little to no attention paid to their needs.

When Jackie provided free childcare so Craig could exercise or have an evening off, she recognized he was facing a huge trial himself as he tried to balance work, travel, wife, kids, and taking care of our home when all the helpers weren't around.

Young children

If the person or family in trial has young children, offering to care for them is another great means of support, especially if the person who is ill can't have them around and/or isn't in a setting where it would be appropriate for them to visit. It's also important to help these precious ones take advantage of every moment they have with their loved one who is ill. If visits are allowed, offer to bring them to the hospital for a short time—making yourself scarce if they need time alone—and then take them home again.

If the person in need has children your own child's age, you could offer to have them over one day a week for a play date, homework, or dinner. Or if you're involved in the same sport or activity, you could sign up to drive them to activities one or more days a week. These gestures would be appropriate if you're Tier 1 or 2, but it's imperative the kids feel comfortable and know you.

Angie thinks the best way to help a parent is to help their child:

I can guarantee the kids are the parents' biggest worry. The goal is to keep things as "normal" as possible for them. No help is as important as inviting that child over for a play date or taking them someplace fun to get them out of the house. If you don't have a relationship with the kids prior to this, find out who does and solicit help from them. Forcing the kids to do things with people they don't know only makes the kids more scared and the parents feel more guilty.

If the ill person is the child, be considerate of their needs, too. Angie said, "Many of our friends were scared of our son after his diabetes diagnosis. They forgot that he was the same boy who wanted to come over to play as before. Even though a parent may need to accompany the child now, invite both parent and child over."

Teens

If kids are older, it's important to discern how you might be available to support them as well. I remember precious moments in the car driving my friend Deborah's teenaged son, John, to and from church or his guitar lessons. He didn't necessarily know me well, but my proximity to their house and my available schedule made me a great choice for this regular task. As the weeks passed, he began to trust me, and we shared some special conversations, although many times we just listened to the radio and didn't talk at all.

What I do know is that by driving John where he needed to go, I freed my friend from worry and stress. When she didn't have the energy to drive because of her chemo, she knew John would get to his regular activities, and his life could go on as normally as possible.

I know of other friends who purposefully got their child placed on the same sports teams with a friend's so they could completely take over the driving to and fro while a parent was ill.

Adult children

Adult children are not to be forgotten. If your friend has college-age or older children, consider sending a care package on behalf of the sick parent. Ask what they like and either compile and send it yourself or help your friend procure all the items needed and ship it off.

If the adult children live on their own, perhaps writing a note to let them know you're thinking of them and praying for them as their parent goes through trial might be just what they need.

Pets

If treatment ensues for a major illness or a family is grieving, pets often suffer from many hours home alone. Most owners would welcome help caring for their pet's basic needs. Making yourself available to walk the dog, clean the cat's litter box, handle daily feedings, or bring their furry friend to your house for a time might be just the thing to help them rest and focus on their stressful situation. And it might not be a detail they've even thought of yet.

When my sister's husband was ill for an extended period of time, she had several neighbors that blessed her with daily dog walks or even with having her dog stay at their house when she and her husband were at the hospital for treatments or away on vacation. I know the doggy caretakers were a huge help to her when she needed to focus on her husband.

Extended family/close friends

My brother Dan died at age 44 of a heart attack. The focus was, of course, on his wife and our mom, but all of his 13 siblings were grieving, too. I will never forget the people who saw my grief. Several drove from long distances to attend the funeral. Others sent beautiful cards to my home. Looking beyond the primary person affected is such a gift to those others who are hurting.

When my friend Kelley passed away, I did all I could to serve her husband, kids, and extended family. Several of us were in charge of the visitation and the funeral arrangements as well as the fellowship following both events. I was honored to be asked to help and considered it a holy privilege to walk alongside their family in that time. But I admit, it was challenging, because we were grieving too.

Initially, I didn't have time to grieve for my friend. But as the dust began to settle and normal life attempted to assert itself, a friend showed up unannounced at my door holding a beautiful blue and pink hydrangea plant. She simply said, "I'm thinking of you and how sad you must be at the loss of your friend. This is for you."

As quickly as she arrived, she was gone.

That gesture of kindness spoke deep to my soul. It was one of the few things I remember of those challenging days following Kelley's death. I also received a card from a different friend telling me how sad she was for my loss and how much she appreciated all that I had done in the years I served my friend and her family through her illness.

> *When you love and serve not just the affected party but also those who are surrounding them each day, your help is multiplied.*

Friends, if you look beyond the obvious you will see many people in the wake of a trial who are just as sad, confused, hurt, lonely, or grieving as the afflicted one—people who are often forgotten. When you love and serve not just the affected party but also those who are surrounding them each day, your help is multiplied. Not only are you touching those who might be overlooked, you are also helping the person directly in trial because you are bolstering their support system!

Chapter 14

nourish normal

Humility is not thinking less of yourself, it's thinking of yourself less.
–C.S. Lewis

during the last few weeks before my due date, while still on bed rest, the doctor told me I could go on one outing a day. I remember looking forward with great anticipation to watching my kids, ages four and two, at their swimming lessons.

On many days, previous to my temporary incapacitation, I dreaded those hectic afternoons—pressed for time, sweating bullets in the tropical temps of the indoor pool, trying to get unruly toddlers to comply. Sadly, I wished those afternoons away in favor of two kids tucked snugly in their beds napping with a moment of peace for me. But once I was unable to participate in the ordinary routine of those frenzied days, oh how I wanted to be a normal mom who wasn't stuck in her bed for 11 weeks. A normal mom who could just take her kids to swimming.

So imagine my excitement when I was allowed to go! Only I couldn't lift my kids. Or help them get dressed. Or hoist them into their car seats to take them to the pool.

Enter: Faithful Mother-in-law.

She came to our house, drove us all there, changed the kids into their suits, escorted them to the right lanes, waited for them to finish, showered them, and wrestled their sticky, wet limbs into dry clothes. All so I could sit in a wobbly, uncomfortable, white plastic chair and be a Normal Mom for 30 minutes.

Some gifts are profound; others may seem more trivial. But those small snippets of normal my friends and family gave to me made a big difference to this weary mom who longed for the tiny blessing of getting splashed by a crew of rambunctious tots practicing their big kid kicks.

Underwater

Once the initial shock of a life-changing situation has worn off, there seems to be a period of time where people grow tired of talking about their problem all the time. I'm certainly not suggesting they are ignoring it, but their reality has changed, and it's hard to live in crisis mode permanently. Things aren't going to be easy—potentially for a very long time. So the best gift you can give that person is some normal in their life.

Imagine your friend immersed in a pool of water all day long. They would be a shriveled mess of wrinkly hands and skin, and they would likely be thinking, "I can't wait to get out of this water!" The water might be freezing cold or annoyingly hot or, at the very least, just plain wet (which is fine for a time, but all day?) And no matter how hard they tried, they could not climb out of the water.

This is similar to the plight of the person in trial. Their own harsh reality is with them every minute of every single day. So your innocent, "How's the water?" could become the iceberg that sank the Titanic. As we've talked about, keeping your mouth shut is a reflection of your ability to put your friend's needs above your own. You may fear they'll think less of you if you don't ask about their situation, but I remind you, it's not about you! You don't need to talk about their trial every single time you see them.

If you're at a baseball game and their child is on your child's team, talk baseball, not cancer. If you're at the office and they work with you, discuss something humorous you did last weekend. If you're at the bus stop, talk about the weather. Cliché, I know, but your simple, normal conversation allows a small sliver of time for them to talk about what they used to talk about *before* such and such happened to them.

It's not only crazy-hard to live in their reality, it's exhausting when every darn person you see constantly wants to talk about *it*. Do not underestimate the power of helping the person you care about feel normal—even if it's just for five minutes. Because you can be certain the water will still be there when you're not. And you don't need to be their iceberg today.

Help Them Find Normal

Angie faced her own cancer and her son's diabetes simultaneously. She said, "One of the more isolating things about a devastating diagnosis is that the rest of the world goes on as normal. Be aware that a 'normal day' is really all that the person wants right now, and anything you can do to preserve or foster normalcy is a true gift."

The people I interviewed who endured extended care needs or long-term trials resoundingly agree—normal is a priority. It's also easily taken for granted. Consider that for many this trial is like moving to another country instead of visiting it for a week. While it's good to be helpful—and sensitive—it's also important to treat the person as you otherwise would. When you promote routine, they might adjust more easily to living in their strange new world.

So invite them to dinner just like you would if their loved one wasn't sick. Ask them to participate in things you have always done together: coffee dates, movies, dinner, concerts, workouts, book club, socializing after work. Crack jokes, talk about everyday things, or ask about areas of their life other than the difficult situation. All these small things help foster a sense of normal. The person you love who has just been diagnosed or has a new circumstance doesn't want to be treated differently because of it. They are still the same person you had a relationship with before.

A few ways to help preserve pockets of normalcy are:

- ✓ Make a special effort to bring the person in trial to their kids' sporting events or activities—even if you need to pick them up and/or leave early.
- ✓ Continue social activities like coffee dates—even if it means bringing the coffee to her.
- ✓ If you are a family member helping out at the house, do the monotonous work, like laundry or dishes. This conserves the parent's time and energy for normal activities, like reading bedtime stories with the kids or sitting at the table for a family meal.
- ✓ Maintain your exercise routine with them—even if the workout length or activity needs to be modified. If exercise isn't possible, honor that time slot and do something else together instead.

"I just want to go to Target."
Kelley courageously battled leukemia for five years. Faced with countless treatments resulting in repeated hair loss, she struggled to find normal

with a bald head. She would wear hats or scarves, but try as you might, sometimes it's hard to hide that you're a cancer patient.

Kelley once told me, "I just want to go to Target and be normal. I don't want the person behind me in the check out lane or the cashier to stop me because I'm bald and tell me a story of a person they know who has cancer too. I just want to get my groceries or my kid's birthday party gift without having to be reminded about my cancer."

When you have cancer, everything changes. When you lose someone you love, everything changes. When you get divorced, everything changes. When your child is sick, everything changes. When you're caring for your aging parent, everything changes. But the person you care for was someone else before this crisis or life-altering event happened. So don't make the mistake of defining them solely by their trial.

> *The person you care for was someone else before this crisis or life-altering event happened. So don't make the mistake of defining them solely by their trial.*

event happened. So don't make the mistake of defining them solely by their trial. They will quickly crumble under the crushing weight of it all if we make them talk about it everywhere they go. Sometimes they want to forget their reality and go to Target like everyone else.

Nourish normal wherever possible, and the person you care about who's facing trial will be grateful you didn't make it about *such and such*—at least for today.

Chapter 15

shine the light

You are the light of the world . . . let your light
shine before others, that they may see your good
deeds and glorify your Father in heaven.
–Matthew 5:14, 16a NLT

for 11 harrowing and frustrating weeks, I was held hostage in my own room on doctor-prescribed bed rest as I awaited the birth of our third child. One day, my neighbor Pam stopped by to see me. As many had done before her, she pulled the visitor chair to the side of my bed. But I wasn't prepared for what came next.

"Do you mind if I pray for you?" she gently asked.

At the time, I knew God but had yet to fully comprehend the person and deep love of Jesus or to walk with Him by my side daily.

In other words, I wasn't totally down with this praying-out-loud thing, much less with someone touching me while they did so. But when she asked, I didn't know how to say, "No, I'm not used to this. How does this even work?"

You could say I was trapped. Or you could say God had me right where He wanted me.

Pam sweetly—and in my mind, bravely—laid her hand on my leg, bowed her head, and began to pray *out loud* over me and my unborn child. (Have I mentioned I was freaking out?!)

What happened next?

I cried my stinking eyes out the whole time she prayed.

You see, God's presence was all over that room and that friend. He used the Holy Spirit living in her and her obedience to do what God asked to give me what I needed. In her humility, she spoke with every day words to the One who was bigger than both of us. Her love covered my discomfort, leaving in its place a teary-faced soul yearning to understand more fully this kind of love and power.

It started with a willing walk between our two houses—across ten yards of grass.

When Pam offered that prayer, I wasn't walking with Jesus. But her prayer became an essential step in my journey toward a new life in Christ. Whether your "neighbor" knows Christ or not, you can be the kind of friend Pam was to me. You can step into the darkness and usher your friend into the light that comes from knowing Jesus, and knowing He is with us in the hard things of life.

Shining in Darkness

Jesus told us that in this life we would have trouble. (John 16:33) Trouble can come in the form of cancer, alcoholism, death, divorce, or any other debilitating trial, and I'm quite sure we all know someone facing those trials. We can't escape it. But if we look, we will see a holy opportunity to witness the display of God's glory in and through it.

There should be a recognizable difference between how faith-filled believers respond to trial compared to how those outside the faith respond. (I will cover ways to minister to those who don't share your faith in Chapter 22.) As we try to come alongside our neighbors of faith through their trials, it's a precious chance to shine the light of God in their darkness. You can become part of His holy kingdom of warriors fighting for His precious ones to remain close to Him and be reminded of who they are and all they have in Christ, as opposed to the temporary trials of earth. Think of yourself as a flashlight illuminating the darkened path of your friend. When they cannot see, you will be there to help them find their way. Because sometimes they cannot see for themselves.

> *Think of yourself as a flashlight illuminating the darkened path of your friend. When they cannot see, you will be there to help them find their way.*

Never underestimate the power of prayer. It is a lifeline, and you may be among the few who are willing to open your mouth and usher someone to the throne of God's grace and love. And don't be someone who just says "I'll pray for you." If possible, do it right then and there!

If you think of someone's journey through trial as a highway, imagine prayer as the rest stop. Maybe you're not able to travel the whole way with them, but you can provide refreshment for a short time along their route. We will cover more about prayer in the next chapter, so stay tuned.

Engage in the Hardship

As discussed at length in Chapter 7: Be Present, often our friends want only our presence, not our empty words or fixes. In his article, "8 Simple Words to Say when Someone You Love is Grieving" on upworthy.com, Tim Lawrence writes:

> I've grieved many times in my life. I've been overwhelmed with shame so strong it nearly killed me. The ones who helped—the only ones who helped—were those who were simply *there*. I am here—I have lived—because they chose to love me. They loved me in their silence, in their willingness to suffer with me and alongside me. They loved me in their desire to be as uncomfortable, as destroyed, as I was, if only for a week, an hour, even just a few minutes. Most people have no idea how utterly powerful this is.

If Jesus is in you, you take Him wherever you go—even if you don't utter a syllable. Sometimes your presence can shine His light even more than your words. Remember our friends in the book of Job. They entered into Job's pain with their presence and silence for seven days. There can be holiness in hardship. Be willing to enter in.

Help Them Focus on God

When crisis erupts, we don't always see clearly. Even if we have an amazing faith, trial can spark doubt, disbelief and uncertainty. Depending on the trial, you may have to remind the suffering person of their identity in Christ as opposed to what the world, or their own mind, is saying about them.

Continual reminders of God's truth come in many forms. You can pray, text, call (if you leave a message, make it clear that a call back is not necessary), send cards or notes. You can also offer encouragement through faith gifts like those we discussed in Chapter 11: Give Good Gifts.

Any reminder of Whose they are instead of what their current circumstance is can be a powerful weapon against the lies of the enemy.

Take a Risk

If you're a person of faith, you might feel a prompting to do something out of your "comfort zone"—even when the person in trial is also a person of faith. Not long after I came to a renewed faith, I felt the Lord asking me to go pray with my mom's aunt, a Catholic nun! She was in the hospital, away from all her loved ones and her community.

I remember sitting in my minivan in the hospital's parking garage asking God for the courage to pray because I felt inadequate. Scared out of my mind, I went inside anyway. In the end, God provided not only the words but also the perfect timing for us to pray (and the guts to kick the doctor out).

> *Even people with deep faith can use an injection of faith from others as they face trial.*

Even people with deep faith can use an injection of faith from others as they face trial. To borrow the words from one of my favorite Christian musicians, Bebo Norman, "When your hope is gone, you can borrow mine."

Be that person who's willing to lend your light and faith at all times, in all situations. Because when you shine your light for others to see, you become the hands and feet of Jesus in a broken and hurting world.

Chapter 16

pray diligently

Be cheerful no matter what; pray all the time; thank God no matter what happens. This is the way God wants you who belong to Christ Jesus to live.
–1 Thessalonians 5:17 MSG

the moment she uttered her first syllable I realized her voice was different. Most of the time she had a brave, positive air. But not that night.

It was peaceful and still, around 10 p.m. Kelley was done being poked, prodded, and visited. I was finished with whatever part of my kids' bedtime ritual I was able to partake in. Over those months when we were both infirm—she in the hospital undergoing another cancer treatment, me laid up in bed recovering from yet another back surgery—we talked on the phone. Those nightly conversations were a highlight of my day. Mostly we caught up on what was happening in our lives because I wasn't able to visit her in person. Other times we commiserated about our latest health woes.

But that night, after I said hello, she spoke tentative, heartfelt words that remain as clear to me now as if the ten years since haven't passed. "I didn't want to call you because I'm feeling really down. I am fighting it. I don't want to pray. I know I should, but I can't. I just don't feel like it. So would you pray for me?"

It's Worth the Effort

That night I prayed because Kelley didn't feel like she could. But there have been countless times when I was on the receiving end of prayer instead.

When I was laid up awaiting my third back surgery, I received a call that my dad died. I lived in another state, apart from my whole family, and I was crushed that I couldn't hop in the car and drive there be with them. I craved comfort and consolation in my grief, but I was depleted physically, mentally, and emotionally. I didn't know what to do, so I started calling my trusted friends from church. Call after call, I asked each of them to pray for me because I couldn't. With each of their prayers, peace started to replace my despair, and solace became my companion.

I kept asking and they kept on praying—until my cup overflowed.

For some people, prayer comes naturally. Others have to work hard to not leave the praying to others. About now you might be thinking, "I'm not a pray-er. I'll skip this chapter, there's lots of other ways I can help!" But I urge you to stay with me. If you've not prayed out loud or prayed silent but specific and intentional prayers for the people in your life facing trial, you haven't experienced the best of what God has for you—or them.

Listen in, friends. Whether you're a sold out pray-er, a wannabe pray-er, or an I'm-not-so-sure-about-this-praying-thing gal, prayer is where the helping gets *holy*.

There are two reasons praying with and for the person facing trial is completely worth it.

> *Prayer is where the helping gets* **holy**.

1. You will be among the few, not the many.
If you are willing to faithfully pray for a person in need, and even voice your prayer *out loud*, you will not just be entering sacred territory, you will begin to walk the road less traveled.

Many people are quick to bring a meal, send a card or note, even drive a kid to dance or football practice. Far fewer are willing to humbly come into the presence of God through prayer alongside the person who's in trial. Jesus told his disciples, "The harvest is plentiful but the workers are few." (Matthew 9:37, NIV) You want to be among the few on this one. I promise.

2. You will be part of God's presence on earth.
There are few ways that bring more of heaven down to earth than talking to God on behalf of someone else in prayer. When Jesus taught His disciples, and by way of that, teaches us, how to pray through what we now call the Lord's Prayer, He said, "Thy kingdom come, thy will be done in earth, as it is in heaven." (Matthew 6:10 KJV)

When we pray, we ask God to bring heaven into this hard place on earth and to bring forth His kingdom and will. This is holy and necessary and life-changing for everyone involved, even when we don't get the answers our flesh desires.

Never have I risked more or been more rewarded than by praying with those who are facing difficult circumstances. This is not to say I haven't had my share of fear or unwillingness. Believe me, I have! But as someone who's been on the other side of those prayers in my own trials, I'll tell you that nothing is more worthwhile than shepherding a loved one in prayer to the throne room of grace.

6 Golden Rules of Prayer

1. Don't just say it, pray it.

"The prayer of a person living right with God is something powerful to be reckoned with." (James 5:16b MSG)

Be the real deal. Don't just say you'll pray for someone; do it. Pray right then, out loud or by whatever means is available to you in that moment—phone, text, email—so they know you are standing in the gap and interceding on their behalf.

Prayer is the most transformative tool I have in my box as I walk out loving my neighbor in their trial. It still doesn't always come as first nature, but it does harness the power of God to minister to people more than any other action in this book.

I have prayed with friends right after a loved one died, when I didn't know what else to do. I have prayed with family after they've received life-altering diagnoses. I have prayed with kids after their parents have died. I have prayed with parents when their child has been in the hospital.

Each time, I felt the holiness.

Each time, the praying changed me.

Each time, I recognized it had nothing to do with me and everything to do with harnessing the power of God and the Holy Spirit.

Each time, I know it's the very best I have to offer—even when I can't fix someone's heartbreaking situation.

2. There's more than one way to skin a cat.

There are several methods you can use to pray with someone. Even though I mentioned praying out loud, if you aren't able to be with the person in person (or you're still working up the courage), you still have options! (Darn, huh?) Each of these prayer methods have been effective for me at various times and places in my life.

- ✓ In-person, out loud prayer (hands on, optional)
- ✓ Community prayer service/corporate gatherings of prayer
- ✓ Small, private prayer groups with extended family/friends
- ✓ Texted prayers
- ✓ Emailed prayers
- ✓ Handwritten prayers in cards
- ✓ Phone call prayers (spoken out loud or left on voicemail)
- ✓ Scripture verse sharing as a form of prayer (by text, email, card)

Personalize your praying method based on what's most comfortable to you and what you will follow through on. If prayer is new to you, start small, then try to stretch yourself and branch out to try different methods over time.

3. Keep your eyes on the road.

Prayer is only effective if we do it! The road of life is busy, and we can miss what we're not looking for. Watch for opportunities to bring the soothing balm of prayer, the hope and joy of God's word, the power of His word spoken over others.

It's also important to be mindful of the faith journey of the person in trial. There will be those you are called to pray for who don't share your theology, denomination, or faith. Simple prayers or Scripture verses are safest. Keep their faith perspective at the top of your mind so you can be honoring and loving instead of offensive or insensitive.

It's important to note that just because someone doesn't have the same outward faith as you, you cannot assume they have no faith.

Tread lightly, knowing God is big enough to take care of what needs taking care of! Your job is to be obedient to whatever He asks you to do.

Keep your eyes on God and give Him glory by interceding on someone's behalf instead of using prayer as a means of changing someone's viewpoint to match your own. You can play a key role in bringing hope and truth through prayer, but it has to be handled with grace and respect.

4. Practice. Practice. Practice.

Internationally renowned priest and author of over 40 books, Henri Nouwen said, "The only way to pray is to pray, and the way to pray well is to pray much." Just like muscles atrophy if they aren't used, so it is with prayer. If your prayer muscles aren't already strong, that's all the more reason to get busy building them up. When you're strong, you're more willing to pray when a need arises.

I remember a time in my life when I would listen to other people pray and think they were "super pray-ers." Translation: They prayed awesome prayers, and I would never have their talents in the prayer department.

Now I now know there is no one kind of "good" pray-er. God hears all our prayers, eloquent or fumbling, rote or heartfelt, humble or proud. He simply wants us to come before Him and speak whatever is on our heart, mind, and soul. And the very best way to improve our comfort in and desire to pray is to come before God in prayer as often as we can.

I learned to pray by doing it—even when it felt awkward or uncomfortable. I spent eight years attending a weekly Moms in Touch (now Moms in Prayer) group, praying for my kids' school. I went to weekly Bible study where we prayed out loud at the end of class. I hosted and attended prayer groups even before I knew what I was doing. I listened, learned, and internalized God's word and His attributes until I could pray without thinking about what I was supposed to say or caring how I sounded to others.

When Kelley was sick, I was put to the test in the prayer department. The first week she was diagnosed, I led a prayer meeting at our church. People came deeply saddened and shocked at her diagnosis of terminal leukemia at such a young age. I was put in the position of leading the group in prayer. Gulp. I didn't think I could do it. But I trusted that those muscles I'd been exercising would hold up. And God equipped me. Because in the end, it wasn't about me or my eloquent words. It was about opening myself up to the vulnerability of prayer by allowing God to work through me.

I will never have the perfect words. Never. But I do feel more confident praying out loud now than I did 14 years ago. And if you practice, over time, so will you.

5. Keep on keeping on.
Whether the opportunity to pray arises once a day, once a week, or once a month, there is something to be said for consistent prayer. Don't underestimate the power of regular, repeated praying for the person facing trial.

> *Don't underestimate the power of regular, repeated praying for the person facing trial.*

A friend shared with me that during her cancer treatments one of her friends texted a prayer every single week, along with verses of encouragement, written prayers, and reminders he was thinking of her. His steadfast dedication of weekly remembrance impacted her. There are times you cannot be present physically, but through prayer and regular contact, you will be with them more than you know.

Prayer is a powerful intervention tool, but it doesn't have to be waved as a banner of "look at what I am doing for you." God knows your heart, hears your prayers, and listens, whether the person you are praying for knows you are praying or not. Jesus said, "But when you pray, go into your room, close the door and pray to your Father, who is unseen. Then your Father, who sees what is done in secret, will reward you." (Matthew 6:6 NIV) There are times to share you're praying for a person but also times to pray and keep it between you and God.

6. Saddle up.

John Wayne is quoted as saying, "Courage is being scared to death but saddling up anyway." No matter how familiar or practiced I become, praying with someone in need still comes with a bit of fear. Less so if I know them well, but if God asks me to step out of my comfort zone, then I gotta say, I'm with the Duke.

I hate to miss any prayer opportunity God presents, but there have been countless times I haven't had the guts to even go near the horse. On the very same day I was working on this chapter of the book, I ran into a friend and learned her husband had been hospitalized because of a life-threatening situation. I listened to all she was experiencing.

How terrible her last few weeks had been! I offered a meal and, of course, my heartfelt empathy. And then I realized I needed to offer the very thing I had spent the better part of the day writing about: prayer! I thought to myself, *I should pray out loud with her. Right here, right now. But I have so much to do, and I need to get home. And what if she thinks I'm weird?*

Ever been there?

I only had a few moments to make my decision. Would I be among the few who offer hope in the form of prayer? Or would I just say, "I'll pray for you" and go on my merry way?

Mentally, I slapped myself upside the head. *Sarah Beckman, you literally just wrote about this very thing today. Now cut the nonsense and get to the praying!*

After all that internal arguing, I finally opened my mouth and offered to pray with her. Believe it or not, the place where we were standing cleared of all people, and we were alone. We sat down, and I asked if I could put my hand on her. Instead of replying, she grasped both my hands. While I prayed for her family, just like so many years ago when my friend Pam prayed for me, I could sense my friend's tears as I spoke.

God was there. With us. In the midst of the terrible, tragic, and terrifying present. And he will also be there with us in the unpredictable future. He will always be where two or more gather in prayer in His name. (Matthew 18:20) That's why we must be willing to saddle up and pray.

Chapter 17

make them laugh

I know not all that may be coming,
but be it what it will, I'll go to it laughing.
–Herman Melville

We were sitting by the pool, a small reprieve before the demands of an upcoming conference. I was interviewing my colleague and treasured friend Michele, gleaning her insights for my book. She'd had her share of hardship—divorce, single parenting, repeated bouts with cancer. She knew trial. She'd lived through many.

"What was helpful to you in the face of your trials?" I asked.

She responded immediately. "Laughter." Followed quickly by, "Stay positive and don't panic."

That spring day we couldn't know that eight months later her cancer would return. And because she had said laughter spoke louder to her than other medicines, I knew exactly what to do.

Unbeknownst to her, I emailed our colleagues all over the country and asked them to be part of a secret effort for our treasured friend. I called it The Make Michele Laugh Challenge. (Of course, now that she's written the foreword for this book, my secret is out. But don't let that stand in your way of attempting to do this without the person's knowledge. She didn't know until I told her three years later!)

The Make 'Em Laugh Challenge

So what does a Make 'Em Laugh Challenge look like? You can organize your group however suits you best—by email, letter, text, or in person. Simply let people know you're trying to make this person's day brighter with laughter. The goal is to be sly, so the recipient doesn't know it's a concerted effort. This approach works even if you aren't in the same town or city as the person you want to uplift!

Here is a generic version of the email I sent. You can adapt and use it according to your needs:

Dear Friends,

I am writing to ask you to partake in a "Make (insert name here) LAUGH Challenge" over the next several months.

Here's how it works:

You will be assigned a specific week below. Your "Make _____ Laugh" event can be completed any time during that week. He/ She will not be aware we are doing this . . . although they might catch on eventually. Your way to make 'em laugh—and the delivery method—are up to you, but here are a few ideas:

Delivery method: Snail mail, email, voicemail, text, telegram, singing telegram . . . whatever makes them laugh! Try not to use social media or your effort might get lost in the shuffle of many other online messages. I'd love for _____ to have a concrete, tangible something from you to save or keep if possible.

Ideas: Knock knock jokes, funny story, humorous memory, silly email chain letter, photo, poem, YouTube video, funny photo, blog post, old videos, book . . . anything funny goes!

Schedule: I'm assigning you dates so it actually happens and our humorous anecdotes don't all arrive at once. (Follow this with names and weeks pre-assigned)

If you can participate, great! If not, no worries. If you don't get it done in your "assigned" week and still feel inspired to share something, please do so whenever you are able. The schedule is just a suggested guideline so our efforts are staggered. As you know, his/ her journey will be a marathon, not a sprint.

I hope you will consider taking a few minutes to brighten our friend's day in the midst of this trial.

Thanks for your time. Laugh on!

It's easier than you think to organize this kind of effort, and the results will be well worth it. My team of folks rose to the occasion. Here are a few of the ways they reached out to Michele:

✓ Emergency nap kit (for help with the young ones)
✓ Old vinyl record (Think Jimmy Fallon "Do Not Play List" segment)
✓ A child's toy with humorous note
✓ Custom t-shirt that mocked the circumstance
✓ A humorous book
✓ A personalized video
✓ A letter with a funny story recaptured

✓ An old photo
✓ A flash mob

Your Make 'Em Laugh campaign will be unique to you or your circumstances. The point is to be intentional in administering the medicine of laughter to a friend in need. Which brings us to the next piece of advice.

Know Your Audience

The Bible says, "A cheerful disposition is good for your health; gloom and doom leave you bone-tired." (Proverbs 17:22, MSG) The most important part of using laughter as a strategy to help your friend in need is to pay attention to their cues. In other words, if they laugh a lot, tell jokes about their situation, or make others laugh often, then you will know your friend would welcome this type of encouragement. Take the cue and run with it!

In the midst of crushing reality, sometimes all you can do is laugh. After her brain cancer diagnosis, Susie from Rwanda kept things light by making jokes to doctors, nurses, family, and friends. She made me LOL (laugh out loud) when she sent this tidbit to me: "Let me tell jokes about death. Let me make lists of who my hubby is and is not allowed to marry. Don't freak out when I tell you I don't wear sunscreen or do breast self-exams because I'm rolling the dice on breast and skin cancer."

Even when Kelley was in the hospital with a feeding tube and all sorts of gadgets and gizmos attached to her, she maintained her witty sense of humor. I walked in one day and asked if she needed anything. She quickly wrote on her white board, "A steak please."

Sometimes we need laughter to take our minds off the harsh reality we are facing. But in all these cases, the laughter began with the "patient" or the person facing trial. Follow cues toward humor, if they are given. If not, find other ways to help.

Watch Out

Pat from Minnesota was hurt when people made light of her mother's Alzheimer's. "As my mom was dying of Alzheimer's, sometimes people would think they were helping lift the grief by 'joking' about things Alzheimer's patients do. I knew they were well intentioned, but their insensitivity made me want to defend and protect the dignity of my mom."

> *Follow cues toward humor, if they are given. If not, find other ways to help.*

Not everyone wants to laugh about the dire situation they face. If you're unsure at all if laughter is the right way to go, then don't go there. You never want to hurt a person by trivializing the situation when you could choose a better way to show your support.

Laughter can be good medicine, but only in proper dosages! Your best guide as to whether or not this method will express love to someone in trial is to pay attention. If you know your friend appreciates your sense of humor or if they lead the way by making jokes themselves, then you know you can walk down the road of laughter.

tap into your talents

From Him the whole body, fitted and knit together by every
supporting ligament, promotes the growth of the body for building
up itself in love by the proper working of each individual part.
–Ephesians 4:16 NLT

W hen Kelley was about three years into her cancer journey, she faced challenging side effects of her many treatments—not the least of which was that she felt constantly cold. One day she told a mutual friend Barb how she loved to take baths to warm up at night. Then she said, "But I don't enjoy being in my bathroom because it's so outdated. I wish I had remodeled it before all this happened."

What you don't know about my friend Barb is that she is a phenomenal decorator, designer, and project manager. She also loves shopping for gorgeous things at great prices and has a giant servant's heart. Her brief conversation with Kelley became the spark that ignited one of the most amazing projects I've ever been part of.

Barb secretly asked Kelley's husband if we could undertake a surprise bathroom remodel to bless Kelley with a tranquil place to restore after what were almost always hard days. He granted his permission—and his checkbook—for us to completely gut and renovate her bathroom.

But here's the kicker: in order to surprise her, we decided to pull off this feat in four days, while Kelley and Randy were out of town. It was the classic *While You Were Out* television show scenario, only we didn't have a giant crew of professionals on our payroll!

What we did have was worth far more. We had a dedicated, loving, selfless collection of friends and family within our church community who volunteered their time and unique talents to serve someone who needed encouragement in the face of a long trial. It's hard to even put into words the depth of love and beauty that came from each person using his gift to complete this project.

As the project manager, Barb corralled people uniquely gifted to cover every area of our remodel, even though none of us worked in professions involving carpentry, remodeling, building, or decorating! From dumpster donation, demolition crew, video editing and photography (we captured the whole project to show Kelley later), wall prep and painting, tile laying, grouting, plumbing, electric wiring, shopping, cabinet and shower installation, to decorating the finished product, well over 25 people contributed their talents.

Kelley and Randy returned around midnight on day four to find a few of us hiding in her bathroom to unveil the surprise. I will never forget her shock and joy! She was overwhelmed and delighted that she now had a peaceful respite where she could soak in her tub with beauty surrounding her. Not to mention that she would think of the profound love that went into creating her oasis every time she stepped foot into her newly remodeled bathroom.

The Perfect Fit

God's word says each part of the body is unique, none being greater than another. All are necessary for the body to function in harmony. (1 Cor. 12:12-27) This project was a roaring success primarily because of the way God brought each person's unique talent and skills together to work as the Body of Christ to bless our friend in her time of trial. It was a privilege to be part of something that demonstrated what this biblical principle looks like in action.

When we use our talents to uplift and strengthen someone in the face of trial, *it is good*. As in when God created the plants and earth and sky in Genesis 1 and He finished and said, "It is good." That's the kind of good I'm talking about.

God uniquely created you and me. He wove into each of us beautiful talents and abilities, according to His perfect grace. We can use, and therefore grow them, or we can let them become stagnant. The beauty comes when we use our giftedness to bless someone in trial. Each time I've seen this in action, it makes me want to shout for joy!

We can use our spiritual gifts, talents, or abilities for lots of pursuits in this life—money, happiness, entertainment, recreation, vocation, ministry. But when we use what God has so perfectly placed in us for the benefit of someone in trial, He multiplies our efforts. And the recipient will feel the goodness in the best kind of loving-your-neighbor way.

I used to think I had to serve in areas I wasn't particularly good at in order to become more sacrificial or humble—more holy. But I have grown to recognize that God's greatest desire is for us to serve our church, our neighbors, and our world in the way He innately created and wired us to serve!

> *God's greatest desire is for us to serve our church, our neighbors, and our world in the way He innately created and wired us to serve!*

Before you get all "we all have to be willing to scrub the floors and toilets" on me, hear me out. Yes, we will be asked to do some tasks that aren't in our natural skill set or that aren't very high on our list. And we should step up when those needs arise. (If your skill is cleaning toilets, I'll let you have that one if you want.) But if we are characterized by (meaning we do these things more often than not) doing tasks outside our God-wired abilities, not only will we be miserable, but others around us will be too.

God created the perfect equation: His gifts bestowed on each of us plus our full use of them equals blessing for everyone—including us! I know it sounds simple. That's because it is. We complicate the matter more than we ought.

Additionally, enlisting others to do what they're good at frees us from the misconception we have to do everything for our friend or loved one. So reach out to family, friends, or your church community and put their talents to work. By doing so, you will live out the Scripture that says every part of the body is necessary to fulfill God's purposes.

Do What You Do Well

When someone you love is facing a trial, one of the first questions you should ask yourself is, "What do I do well that could be beneficial to my neighbor in trial?" When you answer this question honestly (i.e. you don't get to say you have no talent), you will be on your way to discovering how to tap into your talents as a powerful means of helping.

Your talent could be hair cutting, massage, music, singing, accounting, organizing, praying, writing, shopping, decorating, landscaping, painting, cleaning, real estate, medicine, graphic design, computer work, technology, building, plumbing, sheet rocking, electric wiring, cooking, baking, counseling, finance, gardening, coaching, project managing, driving, or even errand running. (Hey, no mocking my talent!) This list could go on and on, but I think you get the gist.

When you use your talents to love your neighbor in trial, you'll be in your sweet spot. And the blessing of that will flow into the lives of those you're serving. Below are just a few of many examples where people have used a talent to help someone in need. Hopefully, they will get you thinking about your own talents and spur you on.

- When a friend lost her husband after a long bout with cancer, Holly offered her design services to freshen and redecorate their bedroom, making it a place for her without all the memories of her husband and his long sickness.
- My mom loves to sing and believes strongly in the power of music to minister to people in times of grief. She started a funeral choir at our church when I was a young girl and continues to sing in the "Resurrection Choir" at 88!
- A friend in divorce mediation needed advice on the legal aspect of separating a business, including valuation, and Craig, who had experience with valuation of companies backed by venture capital, walked her through the process.
- When my brother-in-law Tom was in home hospice care, my sister Terry, a hairdresser for many years, made a house call to give him a haircut.
- When Tom's health prevented him from attending a concert he'd been longing to see, my brother-in-law Chris and my nephew Griffin, both talented guitar players, gave Tom an impromptu

concert in the family room, including a valiant effort to play his favorite song by the artist he'd wanted to see!

- My brother-in-law Allen, an ordained deacon in the Catholic Church, and my sister Ellen, a home care/hospice nurse, came several times to minister to Tom spiritually and physically.

- Countless times my friend Heather, a hairdresser and a nurse, has tended those with a debilitating illness by cutting their hair, massaging their feet, giving pedicures, or addressing their needs as a patient with staff or family. She was my go-to gal when I knew either Kelley or Deborah needed blessing in that area. I loved to watch her use her God-given gift of compassion as she loved them in their trial.

- Kris, an accountant, stepped up to help a widowed friend whose husband had handled all the finances learn, manage, and make key financial decisions.

- Friends and neighbors undertook a huge outdoor landscaping project that Eva's husband had started but didn't have time to complete when she faced extended cancer treatments.

- When Kelley was first diagnosed with cancer, friends Alli and Jennifer used their talent for jewelry making to create over 200 prayer bracelets for Kelley's family and friends to wear as a reminder to pray for her.

- Always a lover of tending to her yard and landscaping with great care, Deborah blessed neighbor Kay with a freshly mowed lawn the day of her young nephew's funeral. Many times, Deborah also helped me plant my front flowerbed when my back wasn't up for the task.

- Because of my writing and speaking background, I have been able to deliver eulogies on behalf of several families for their loved ones. Never did I dream my gifts would translate to "eulogist," but to date, I've delivered four.

- When Deborah began her chemo, friends, Basil and MaryJane, offered to be her "delivery service." They showed up every week with the car warmed and ready and drove her to and from her treatments. The car, the time, and the willingness combined to create a unique "talent" which filled an important need.
- After Deborah passed away, one of her backyard neighbors who loved dogs came over at least once a week to play with Deborah's dog. It became a beautiful friendship, which later translated into offers to take the dog to the vet or groomer or to dog sit when the family was away.

Between bed rest and four back surgeries, a multitude of people served me and my family with their talents: folks cooked amazing meals, ran errands, cleaned my house, cared for my kids, cleaned my refrigerator and linen closets, brought me coffee, listened to me, prayed for me, drove me, visited me, loved me, and even birthday shopped for my kids! I'd love to list them all by name, but I know I would inadvertently leave someone out. Even if I can't come up with all their names, trust me—I remember their service. Why?

Because each of them served with great love.

There are countless ways your skills could bless someone in need. I haven't even begun to touch the surface! If you'd like to add your idea or experience to the list, I'd love for you to share it with us on our Facebook Community Page at www.facebook.com/alongsidebook/.

Watching people joyfully serve someone in trial is like unwrapping a much-wanted gift on Christmas morning. There is a great opportunity when talents meet need; and when you're serving in your sweet spot, the fruit of your work is even sweeter. I've found when I'm tapped into my talents I enjoy loving my neighbor even more. I think you'll discover the same—if you haven't already.

Chapter 19

collaborate

For the body does not consist of one member but of many.
–1 Corinthians 12:14 ESV

a s I was writing this book, our beloved former church community in Minnesota experienced a great loss. One of our dear friends suffered a sudden heart attack a week before Christmas. Since I live far away, I felt helpless. I wanted to be with my people doing what we do—loving a neighbor in trial. So I reached out to several close friends to get a sense of how things were going. One friend wanted to know what she should do, and I shared several of the ideas from this book.

Interestingly, not long before this, I had tapped into my friend Dawn's talents as an amazing graphic designer and computer whiz to create personalized Scripture cards for my website. (Download your own at www.sarahbeckman.org/printable-scripture-cards) The electronic file contains verses focused on comfort, hope, and peace, with a spot to insert someone's name in each verse. These cards can then be printed, cut, and given as a special gift of encouragement in the face of trial. I was able to share this file with my friend, who planned to make and deliver them in the following days as an expression of sympathy to the grieving family.

We talked in the previous chapters about using our gifts to help. But in this case, three of us worked together to bless one! This is just one small example of how collaboration can benefit everyone when it comes to loving your neighbor in their trial.

Several days later, I received a message from yet another friend in that community. They had coordinated a candle vigil, where anyone who wanted could leave a candle of their choosing with a short note of love on the front walk of the family's home on Christmas Eve. She kindly offered to help me take part from far away. She not only sent me pictures of candle choices, she also hand wrote my message on the card and delivered it to the house during the scheduled time. I was so honored and grateful to be included from afar!

Our friend who lost her husband later posted a photo online of all the candles on her sidewalk and expressed her gratitude for the outpouring of silent love. This idea was powerful because a large number of people came together to shine light in someone's dark hour.

Expressing Love Together

There are many options to express your sympathy, support, or love as a larger group. As you consider planning a collaborative event, the examples below may help spark your own ideas.

- At Kelley's funeral, her middle son's baseball team showed up in their baseball uniforms to honor their teammate's Mom. When they walked in together, it took people's breath away.
- On the day of a friend's major surgery, her friends and neighbors organized a silent prayer meeting on her lawn. They circled her house with a giant ring of people holding hands and praying. They literally surrounded that family with prayer!
- When my friends' son died, they suggested donations to a local non-profit that packs meals for the hungry because their son had enjoyed serving there. A group of the father's cycling friends later organized a serving day at that charity in honor of his son. He was so moved by the thoughtful gesture, and it meant so much to him when many of the group, along with their families, showed up to serve. They have since made it an annual event.
- When my brother-in-law was fighting melanoma, many people joined him to participate in the Annual Run/Walk for Melanoma in his area. "Team TD" continues to participate in that event each year. My niece, Darby, also founded a bowling event that takes place each December in Tom's memory. Well over 100 people show up not only to raise money for research, but also to demonstrate to my sister and her boys that people still stand with them in their loss.
- Similarly, when Kelley was diagnosed with leukemia, we collectively joined in walking at the Light the Night event to support leukemia/lymphoma. For several years, we participated in the formal event put on by the local chapter.
- One year, Kelley wasn't feeling well enough to do the "big event" so several friends decided to create a satellite event at our local park. They purchased balloons, just like the larger event, and people brought food to share at the park before we walked

around the lake a few miles from Kelley's home. It turned out to be everyone's favorite event, and it became an annual tradition to skip the larger walk and do our own local one instead. This legacy continues through our friend Karen, a 10-year leukemia survivor, who selflessly organizes this event to pay tribute to Kelley and keep fighting for a cure!

- When Dave underwent a bone marrow transplant and had to travel away from home for treatment, his three daughters enlisted friends, family, and acquaintances to write letters to their dad with words of encouragement, prayer, or inspiration. He opened one letter a day during his six-week stay. It was just what he and his wife needed to remain positive and uplifted.

Utilize Existing Resources

We've mentioned a few resources, such as Caring Bridge, already. Others are included in the Appendix. But here is a quick list of people or resources to collaborate with to bring relief to a person or family in crisis.

- ✓ Pastors
- ✓ Professionals: accountants, lawyers, dentists, doctors, therapists, counselors, psychologists, chiropractors, nurses, hospice care
- ✓ Service industry: massage, beauty, household maintenance, landscaping, carpet cleaning
- ✓ Church ministries: meals, prayer, youth, specialized tasks (like car repair)
- ✓ Stephen's Ministry (Stephen's ministers do ministry to those in need, such as terminal illness, loss of a loved one, divorce etc.)
- ✓ Meal coordination websites: Take Them a Meal, Care Calendar, Meal Train, Caring Meals, FoodTidings

- ✓ Meal delivery/grocery delivery services: Hello Fresh, Take Them a Meal, Blue Apron, Amazon Pantry, Amazon Fresh
- ✓ Task oriented websites: Care Calendar, Lotsa Helping Hands
- ✓ Communication/support websites: Caring Bridge, Care Calendar
- ✓ Neighborhood/school groups
- ✓ Church groups/Bible studies/prayer groups
- ✓ Associations/volunteer groups
- ✓ Employers
- ✓ Helplines
- ✓ Support groups

The multiplied impact of many people together versus one person alone can bring even more significant help, hope and encouragement.

The multiplied impact of many people together versus one person alone can bring even more significant help, hope and encouragement to the person you care about who's facing trial. King Solomon in the Bible, known for his wisdom, writes, "And though a man might prevail against one who is alone, two will withstand him—a threefold cord is not quickly broken." (Ecclesiastes 4:12 ESV) Consider how you can join forces with others to make an even greater impact as you love your neighbor in trial.

Chapter 20

take care of you

Cast all your anxiety on him because he cares for you.
−1 Peter 5:7 NIV

a s you may have figured by now, my experience coming alongside my best friend Kelley as she battled leukemia was a major factor in compelling me to write this book. But five long years of being intricately involved in care and concern for Kelley and her family left a huge void in my life after losing her. It was harder than I imagined. For a long time after her death, I tried to deal with it on my own.

On the outside, I continued my regular routine as a mom, wife, volunteer, speaker, and blogger. But on the inside, I was suffering more than I showed. I wrote about it on my blog, but even then, I was guarded. I felt I didn't deserve to grieve as intensely as her family or even

151

other close friends. I felt they had more "right" than I to be sad. In my game of comparative grief, I was the loser because I shoved my feelings aside, trying to keep it all together in the name of pride.

Nine months after Kelley died, I landed in the emergency room. Initially, my symptoms were misconstrued as heart-related because of my brother's early death from a heart attack. After a night in the hospital and a stress test to confirm all was clear with my heart, they sent me home with no answers. It was only after I got some perspective from a friend I suspected I'd had an anxiety attack. I could no longer deny my deep grief over the loss of Kelley. My body was finally crying "Uncle."

Within a week, I had a recommendation for a Christian counselor. My true healing began in her office and continued for months thereafter. Slowly, I found my way back, giving credence to all I'd been through with Kelley as a means to understand how challenging it was for me to let go.

What I learned from this experience was twofold: 1) Never underestimate the power of grief, and 2) No matter how much other people need you, it's of utmost importance to remember to take care of yourself along the way.

During the safety briefing on an airplane, the flight attendant will say something like this: "Should the need for oxygen arise, an oxygen mask will automatically drop down from above you. To start the flow of oxygen, pull the mask toward you, place the mask firmly over your nose and mouth, and breathe normally. If someone near you needs assistance, secure your mask first before assisting the other person."

If I'm honest, I'm really good at securing everyone else's oxygen masks, but I'm not very good at securing my own.

Not everyone has my personality. But if you have a Tier 1 or Tier 2 relationship with someone facing trial, you better be darn sure you take heed of this advice. You may not end up in the ER, but if you're not conscientious about caring for yourself, it will ultimately render you ineffective to care for anyone else.

Rules of Engagement

Maybe you've been helping someone, and you're beginning to feel the stress and strain. Or maybe you are in the preparation stage. No matter where you are, it's essential at this juncture to put on your oxygen mask so you can be effective in the journey ahead.

Take care of you.

This might sound basic, but you probably need to be reminded. It's not selfish to practice self-care when helping someone through a trial. It's of the utmost importance. I repeat, *it's not selfish*! If you need reminding, just reread the words of the flight attendant.

> *It's not selfish to practice self-care when helping someone through a trial.*

How you take care of yourself depends a bit on your personality and what restores and revives you, but most of us will do well to continue things such as regular exercise, eating well, adequate rest, maintaining social activities and time with supportive friends.

If you're a primary caregiver for someone facing illness, start by focusing on self-care for one hour a day, even if you have to break it up. You could give yourself twenty free minutes to sit down for a meal, add in a twenty minute walk, and twenty minutes to sit and be still somewhere away from your "patient." Even in small doses, focusing on you is important.

If you fall into a Tier 1 or 2 category and patient care isn't your primary responsibility, you might still find yourself spending a majority of your free time "loving your neighbor." If so, try to maintain balance so you'll remain a viable source of help. In other words, consider helping for ¼ or ½ of your free time in a given week instead of all your free time.

For example, don't completely give up your regular exercise routine in order to be available, but maybe use one of your allotted exercise slots to help your friend. If there's an acute situation, try to resume your normal exercise as soon as possible in order to stay grounded and healthy throughout the illness. This same rule applies to areas of your life other than exercise. Use it where needed to take care of yourself.

An empty gas tank won't power your car where you need it to go. Likewise, if you don't keep your personal tank full—physically, mentally, emotionally, and spiritually—sooner or later you will end up stalled on the side of the road.

Keep the faith.

It's important to be sure your faith doesn't fade into the background because you're busy caring for a friend or loved one. Don't stop attending church, prayer groups, Bible studies, or discipling/mentoring meetings. Whatever you do to strengthen or build up your own faith life, be sure you keep on doing it. It's imperative to keep your own cup full so you can continue to pour out into others' lives.

Maintain your boundaries.

Are you a compassionate, empathetic, servant-hearted person who will serve anyone and everyone in their time of need? Do you find yourself always serving someone—often at the expense of yourself or even your own family? If this is you, I beg you to slow down and assess how much you're serving others. If an honest evaluation clarifies you are giving too much of yourself away, pull back and practice saying no. It's been said that when you say yes to one thing, you're saying no to something else. Some of us say yes to others and no to our families—or to ourselves.

I am guilty as charged!

There are situations where someone facing trial will be desperate for help, and you will seem like the only person they can turn to. Be wary of those folks who might take advantage of your help, whether they intend to or not. It can happen, so don't be naïve—keep healthy boundaries. If you are prone to "over helping," stay accountable with trusted friends who can help you see the warning signs.

I have learned to set boundaries when it comes to helping a neighbor in trial based on how much my family or my schedule can handle. I can't dishonor one to honor the other, but it's helpful to consider the next point in light of this truth.

Don't try to do it all.

I am not, nor do I have to be, Superwoman. I have limits, and I'd do well to adhere to them. (I haven't forgotten my trip to the ER.) Trying to be someone's "everything" is not only unhealthy, it's impossible! Additionally, taking on every burden for someone else is often achieved at the expense of yourself and/or your family.

Trying to be someone's "everything" is not only unhealthy, it's impossible!

In our earnestness to help, we can also overdo to the point of becoming a burden to the person we intended to bless! Keep your offers and help to a manageable amount and be sure to watch for signs that your help is welcomed or becoming too much. Not sure? Gently ask the person you're helping, giving them full permission to be honest with their response.

Share the load.

When it was difficult for me to accept people's offers of help in my times of trial, my husband would say, "When you say no, you're robbing people of the blessing of helping." It took me a while to fully embrace his wisdom, but now I see the value in it.

This also applies if you are trying to do all the helping. When you do everything yourself, you rob others of the opportunity to serve and to experience the joy and blessing of coming alongside. Additionally, if you're feeling overwhelmed, utilize other people's talents as discussed in Chapter 18: Tap into Your Talents.

If you are in a Tier 1 relationship, it's especially important to remind yourself you aren't their only "someone." This acknowledgment might make it easier for you to allow others to help.

Check your motives at the door.

My last piece of advice for self-care is to be sure you are walking with a pure and upright heart. As we help another in trial, our prayer for ourselves should be, "Create in me a pure heart, O God, and renew a right spirit within me." (Psalm 51:10 NIV)

My friend Susie Albert Miller, an author and speaker who writes about relationships at www.susiemiller.com, has faced great trial in her life with both the loss of a child and chronic illness. In the midst of one such trial, a close friend told her, "I don't need you to need me." I love this statement because it focuses on the motives of the person who is offering support. Susie's friend wanted to be there for her, but was also clear that it was about Susie's needs, not hers. In other words, she wasn't looking to be validated by Susie. This alleviated undue stress on Susie to help her friend feel better when she had a full plate already. This is a perfect reminder of our recurring theme, "It's not about you!"

I am ashamed to say I've been guilty of impure motives. I love to help, and I love the feeling I get when I do. But if my help is more about my feelings of self-worth than about the one I am helping, then I'm helping for all the wrong reasons. Even if my initial motives are pure, this can be a slippery slope. It's easy to fall into helping because gratitude, indebtedness, and praise often follow. Those are weighty outcomes if you're a "helping addict."

I don't use this term in disrespect to other addictions—or even use it lightly. I use it because addiction to helping is a real consideration. I'm sure you probably know people who fall into that category. I know because it takes one to know one.

If "helping addict" characterizes you, please join me in a continual effort toward self-awareness. If helping someone fuels an unhealthy, inflated sense of self-worth, then I suggest you pray earnestly for God to help you arrest this trait in yourself before you serve others.

Self-care isn't just a good idea—it's an essential part of loving someone in trial. If you haven't secured your own mask before the plane loses oxygen, you will be rendered useless to assist others. Don't wait until it's too late. Set healthy parameters from the start for your support and care so that you'll be fit to run the amazing race of loving your neighbor in their trials.

Chapter 21

don't do this . . .

Be the change that you wish to see in the world.
–Mahatma Gandhi

ometimes it is more effective to tell someone what *not* to do.
I intentionally structured the majority of this book using
positive actions as a guide for you to help your neighbor in trial.
However, there were such strong sentiments of those interviewed
about what *doesn't* work or *isn't* helpful that what follows is my best
summation of these facts. Because my interviewees encompassed
various types of trauma, illness, life-change, and duress, this list is
applicable to most trials.

But before you peruse this compilation, hear this: I'm quite sure
every one of us has at one time or another done or said something on

this list. Myself included. Since you can't change the past, the important thing is to learn from your mistakes and not repeat them in the future. Believe me, the person you're trying to help through their trial will be grateful if you heed these warnings.

> *The important thing is to learn from your mistakes and not repeat them in the future.*

The following observations are from real people who have gone through real trials. I didn't assign the ideas to anyone specifically because multiple people said the same thing. This fact makes such advice universally true. Others had unique and lengthier insights which I quote after the general list. And while some of these concepts are covered in the other chapters of this book, it's always good to have a quick reference guide as a place to start—or to return to over and over again.

Complete Guide of What Not To Do

- ✓ Don't bring dishes that have to be returned.
- ✓ Don't look at me with that pitiful look you think is sympathy.
- ✓ Don't give me trivial gift stuff that clutters my counter.
- ✓ Don't panic.
- ✓ Don't gossip about me and my personal health status or information.
- ✓ Don't cry in front of me.
- ✓ Don't try fix or remedy my situation.
- ✓ Don't obligate me to return phone calls.
- ✓ Don't help just to take credit.
- ✓ Don't talk about how much you sacrificed to help me or regale me with your day's to-do list and the fact that you fit me in.
- ✓ Don't talk about my trial every time you see me.

✓ Don't talk too much.

✓ Don't drop off a meal and expect a lengthy visit.

✓ Don't forget my struggle.

✓ Don't make commitments you cannot keep.

✓ Don't be oblivious to my hardship.

✓ Don't speak in sad, piteous tones to me or my loved ones.

✓ Don't make offers that require work on my part or that you can't follow through on.

✓ Don't presume to know my prognosis.

✓ Don't publicly discuss information I haven't made public.

✓ Don't think the rules don't apply to you.

✓ Don't spend time discussing or doing trivial things if the trial is acute, recent, or terminal.

✓ Don't be patronizing or judgmental, especially in delicate situations like abuse, suicide, divorce, or addiction.

✓ Don't share your own story ad nauseam.

✓ Don't be bossy.

✓ Don't take over. (Unless asked.)

✓ Don't say "Let me know if you need anything."

✓ Don't expect a thank you note.

✓ Don't give your medical advice.

Don't look at me like I'm dying.

"My burning advice involves *not* treating the cancer victim (or talking to her) as if she's dying. Ugh. I'm *not* dying, but well-intentioned people use words that make it sound as if I am. It's hard enough to fight the mental battle without that little piece of help. Your tears also make me feel like I'm dying. There's a time for empathy, but I need hope and positivity from you." –Michele from Colorado

Don't offer a home party in my benefit.

"I've experienced a range of pitches offering to help via direct sales schemes. People offer to host a home party for my friends and ask them to buy things so I will get the profits to help me. That sounds nice, but it puts me into a horribly awkward position, and there's no way for it not to come across as very self-serving for the seller. Even if I get the profits from that party, the seller's business benefits from the contact info of all of my friends and the opportunity to turn them into hosts. One person suggested I tell my friends that her products were necessary for my health then ask my friends to 'shower' me with these vitamins I 'needed.' I was so offended at this manipulation I didn't know what to say." –Susie from Rwanda

Don't overstay your welcome.

"Several times people have spent 3 hours+ with me. I absolutely know their hearts were in the most loving place, but I don't recommend it. The 'patient' obviously wants those precious moments with their friend, but truly anything more than an hour should generally be reserved for either close family or at the individual's request. When going through a serious illness, the energy to sustain an engaged interaction just isn't there like it was when they were healthy." –Lora from California

I hope you receive these words of advice in the spirit of love and truth in which they are intended. None of us will be perfect when it comes to walking alongside our neighbor in trial, but knowing the obstacles that could derail our efforts, we'd do well to follow the posted road signs.

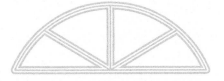

Part 3

special circumstances

"Love bears all things, believes all things, hopes all things, endures all things."
—1 Corinthians 13:7 ESV

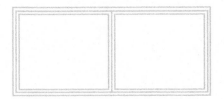

Chapter 22

when faith isn't shared

O n that bright, crisp April day almost a decade ago, I was faced with what felt like a monumental decision—whether or not to cross the street to comfort my neighbor Deborah after her husband, John, died. I knew she'd be leaving for the airport soon because John had been out of town on business at the time of his death. As I stood in the street pondering whether to go to her, I had very little time to act.

I was feeling prompted to go over and pray with her. However, what I knew about Deborah's faith consisted of a few offhanded comments I'd heard through the grapevine—that she didn't attend church regularly and didn't want to be invited. Between that and the fact that I considered myself a Tier 3 friend, the very thought of praying with her gave me great anxiety.

But I knew I couldn't let fear get in the way of what God was asking me to do. I'd been here before, and He hadn't let me down yet.

I made the seemingly endless walk across the street and rang the doorbell. Deborah and her family and a few close friends were in the kitchen getting ready to go to the airport. I hugged her and expressed my sympathy for her loss. Then I stood there for a few minutes trying to gather my nerve. Finally I bumbled, "Would it be okay if I pray for you before you go?"

Oh dear heaven, what was I thinking? Was I really standing here asking to pray out loud with near strangers?

I could sense it wasn't routine for anyone present to be prayed for out loud, and it was moderately awkward. However, I gathered them in a circle and offered a meager prayer of blessing over Deborah's trip and asked for God's strength and comfort in their time of loss. I managed to come through the experience alive.

My prayer wasn't anything earth shattering, but speaking those few words was a giant leap of faith. And I can tell you that God began a wondrous thing that day in spite of my inadequacy and fear. What took place in Deborah's kitchen will remain etched in my memory forever because it was a pivotal day in my quest to understand Jesus' command to love our neighbor. It was also the day I began to learn how to walk alongside someone who doesn't share my faith during her greatest time of need.

When I decided to "go," I could never have known how far reaching the implications would be.

Church Lady

Over the following days and weeks, a few of us church-going neighbors—Kay, Cathy, and I—did lots of things people do when someone dies: cooked, made coffee, cleaned up dishes, made more food, cleaned up more dishes, sat, visited, cried, and consoled. We made photo boards and lists, helped write the obituary, created a funeral program, ordered flowers, bought dark glasses, consulted on funeral clothes. Then we prayed, consoled, and cried some more.

One day we heard Deborah and another neighbor joking about the "Church Ladies." I was quite certain the moniker was not meant as a compliment to those of us transporting vats of coffee and scrubbing the piles of glasses and dishes that mounted in those early mourning days. It was the first time I had ever been called that, but even though we knew we had been made fun of, we kept on making the coffee, bringing food, serving the dinners, doing the dishes, and checking in each day to see what was needed. I bristled at the dig in the beginning, but it didn't take long for me to cherish the title we'd been given.

About a month after John died, after the funeral was over, the visitors had waned, the intensity of details had diminished, the Church Ladies were still there helping Deborah figure out how to live in the face of her new reality.

One day, Deborah turned to me in the hallway of her home. "I need to apologize. I admit we made fun of you for being a *church lady*. But if I had the means, I would buy you a huge diamond necklace to show you how much I appreciate all you've done for me. I will never, ever, make fun of church ladies again. You've made all the difference, and I can never thank you enough."

I didn't need a diamond necklace. What I had just received was far more precious.

We had earned the respect, trust, and gratitude of a woman who needed someone to love her through one of the most challenging moments she had ever faced: the loss of a loved one. We brought faith into the equation, and she couldn't help but notice. And we had done all we could to love our neighbor well.

God knew what he was doing that fateful April day when He sent me across the street to pray in Deborah's kitchen. He knew she would need people around her to shine His light as life continued to get harder. Deborah was diagnosed with breast cancer just two years after her husband died. And two years after that, I sat by her side as she took her last breath.

Four years.

At the beginning, she was an acquaintance.

At the end, a beloved friend.

Intentional Steps to Sharing Faith

When those who don't share our faith go through hardship, we have the opportunity be instruments of God's bigger plan and purpose, opportunity that's wasted if we don't respond.

If my friend Pam hadn't shared her faith with me through prayer, conversation, and encouragement during my bed rest trial, I might never have been in a place to write this book. There is something special about people who are willing to foray into faith matters with those facing crisis who don't claim faith. Again I remind you, the harvest is plentiful, and the workers are few. (Matthew 9:37)

I could write a whole book on the subject of sharing your faith, and many others already have. But for our purposes, the following are several steps you can take as you begin to reach out to a "neighbor" who doesn't share your faith. Intentionality is important. You might be learning as you go, but God will use your willing heart!

Start early.

You never want it to be a surprise to someone that you are a person of faith. If you have a chance to bring up your faith early in a relationship, keep it simple and brief, but get it out there.

Don't be ashamed to mention church, spiritual things, or your faith conversationally. If your friend asks what you're doing and it involves church, say so. Mention Sunday church, Bible study, the youth group you volunteer for, or the mission trip you're going on, but small doses are key. No need for a monologue or dissertation on the woes of the spiraling world and how everyone needs Jesus—just a simple mention of where you're coming from as a baseline for later conversations.

But be prepared. When you open this door, sooner or later they will likely want to come inside! You've let them into your life a little bit, and that's what you want.

Build relationships.

In his book, *Contagious Christian*, Bill Hybels says it takes roughly 20 hours of relationship building with an unbeliever before we earn the right to share one hour about our faith.

20:1.

Relationship is the currency we use to earn our chance to share the goodness of God's grace and redemption with others. Become friends first, share faith later. Bill Hybels writes,

> *Relationship is the currency we use to earn our chance to share the goodness of God's grace and redemption with others.*

You can't be a contagious Christian without getting close enough to other people to let them catch the disease. This is where the whole enterprise is won or lost, at the actual point of contact. Friends listen to real friends. So become one. If we don't start there, we can't effectively get anywhere.

People outside of our Christian faith are not a conquest or conversion opportunity. They should never be viewed as another notch in our belt. They are real people who need to be shown real love in the name of Jesus. Serve in love first, share faith later.

As you venture more deeply into their lives, there will be days you are discouraged and days you are elated. But walking alongside people in regular life gives you the chance to walk alongside them in trial.

Prepare.

You wouldn't go on a journey without a bit of preparation. Likewise, if you hope to share faith with someone in a difficult situation you will need to be prepared. In 1 Peter 3:15, we are told to be prepared to share the reason for the hope we have, and to share that reason with gentleness and respect.

There are several ways you can prepare to share your faith:

1. Pray for the person.

Be in prayer for the people you know who might be un-churched (never been in church) or de-churched (left the church at any age) or even what I call dis-churched (disenchanted with church). Prayer should precede all conversations or interactions when possible!

2. Know your story.

If you have a testimony of how God changed your life, showed up in a trial, or answered your prayers, be sure you have thought through your story or even written it down. Then, if given the chance, you will be ready to share. Focus on what aspects of your story might be similar to what the person is going through, and be sure to highlight the goodness of God as opposed to only talking about the worst parts of your story.

3. Know the gospel.

Many times when people face trial they are more open to conversations of faith than at any other time in their life. Having the ability to verbalize the gospel message is paramount to your ability to help someone if they are ready to receive God's saving grace.

4. Have your go-to.

If you have a favorite faith gift, be sure you keep it on hand. Favorite Bible verses are also good to share, but don't overwhelm. If a faith gift you've used in the past was well received, don't be afraid to use it again.

Angie is an avid lover of her neighbor in trial. She says,

> I've had a couple situations where the family is very resistant to Christianity, so I've gone carefully. But I always include a *Jesus Calling* devotional in my care packages. The entries are spot on and manageable for anyone. You never know if trial will bring someone closer to God or cause them to search for true hope. Those of us who do have faith can best help by sharing our faith, while being sensitive to not forcing it. The message that they aren't alone is so very important.

Look for opportunity.

Recently, I had a client going through some tough times. She didn't seem opposed to the Bible, but I knew by her own admission that she didn't practice Christianity. Because we had a relationship already, I wrote her an email and shared some Scriptures. I said, "As you know, I'm a woman of faith, and as such, I will pray for you in this time. I have a few verses that give me comfort when times are rough. Maybe some of them will help you in whatever context that looks like for you."

I included a few of my favorite comforting Bible verses and links to find them online. I concluded with a general message of encouragement that wasn't "churchy" in any way. She responded with gratitude for my prayers and said she loved the verses!

> *Be faithful to watch for times when God is asking you to shine His light to a hurting soul, and you'll find opportunities everywhere.*

Be faithful to watch for times when God is asking you to shine His light to a hurting soul, and you'll find opportunities everywhere.

Act bravely.

I was drinking coffee with a friend in the afternoon sunshine when I noticed a woman a few tables away. She sat there for at least ten minutes, her whole body shaking, her hands covering her face. She was crying, and she was alone.

I couldn't avert my eyes. It was obvious she was in terrible pain. I didn't want to be rude to the person I was with, as we were deep in our own conversation, but that holy nudge couldn't be ignored. I knew God was telling me to reach out and comfort the crying woman.

Why do I always end up in these now or never moments? I thought. Then I told my friend that I felt like I should go over and pray for her. Without hesitation, she agreed.

I walked over and asked the woman if she was ok. Turns out her boyfriend had died the week before, and it was her first day back at work. She was crushed—and it showed. After listening to her story, I asked if I could pray for her.

Her answer was a resounding yes. We shared a short, quiet prayer right there outside Starbucks before her break ended. She headed back to work, and I returned to my patient friend.

That moment opened the door to a sweet friendship. That woman facing great sorrow was a clerk at the grocery store I frequent. I've seen her many times since and have been able to follow up on how she's faring. Just last week she stopped me after I checked out and gave me a hug.

There are times we will be called upon to love our neighbor in trial—even when that person is a stranger. And when we do, we obey God. "But he's already made it plain how to live, what to do, what God is looking for in men and women. It's quite simple: Do what is fair and just to your neighbor, be compassionate and loyal in your love, and don't take yourself too seriously—take God seriously." (Micah 6:8 MSG)

Let's walk humbly and act bravely in the face of another's need, whether we know the state of their faith or not.

Chapter 23

when you've "been there"

All praise to the God and Father of our Master, Jesus the Messiah!
Father of all mercy! God of all healing counsel! He comes alongside
us when we go through hard times, and before you know it, he
brings us alongside someone else who is going through hard times so
that we can be there for that person just as God was there for us.
–2 Corinthians 1:3-4 MSG

S everal years ago, a friend was facing a terrible circumstance wrought from her husband's alcoholism. Because my father was an alcoholic, I had a sense of the sorrow and trial her family was enduring. I felt a strong stirring to go to her and see if I could offer any encouragement.

When I reached out, she eagerly accepted my offer to visit. I went with a willing heart, not knowing if I was going to share my own story or not but ready to if needed. After lots of listening, I mentioned I would be happy to talk to her children about my own experience with an alcoholic father, if she was open to it. She was! She immediately invited her children downstairs to join us. God showed me just what they needed to hear of my story, and it became a beautiful time of conversation and prayer.

To Share or Not to Share

There are occasions when sharing your own experience is definitely beneficial, and there are times it could be detrimental or taken the wrong way. If you've been in a similar situation to a person or family going through trial, be open if God calls you to share your experience. If you haven't "been there," consider keeping your great wisdom (or God forbid, correction!) to yourself and instead be a listening, supportive friend.

Tier 1 or 2 relationships will provide more opportunity for sharing; however if you're a Tier 3 or 4 and have valuable direct experience to relate, consider finding someone who is Tier 1 or 2 to pave the way by asking if the person is interested in hearing about your experience.

Angie believes in sharing when you've walked the same road and "get" a person's trial:

> I think it is vital to reach out. You don't have to have all the answers, but you can serve as a source who "gets it" and hopefully share what was and wasn't helpful to you. I've learned way more from other moms of diabetics than I've ever learned from my son's specialists. I switched surgeons based on the advice of other women who'd had my same surgery. I bought clothes post-surgery based on the advice of others who knew what

the challenges were. I've gotten some of my best perspective by observing how other faith-filled friends approached their diagnoses. And my husband found more solace in a beer with a friend whose wife also had cancer than he did with any pastor.

If you're called to share from your own trials or experiences, begin with these guidelines.

1. Wait.
Give the person time to digest their situation before diving in with your story or advice. If what you know is time-sensitive, ask before sharing your insights.

2. Seek.
As a Christian, I seek God's wisdom and trust the Holy Spirit to guide me as to if and when to I'm supposed to share my own journey with someone. If He wants you to share, trust Him to also grant you opportunity. I also pray for a willing and obedient heart, especially if the situation is complicated or messy.

3. Listen.
Do lots of listening before you begin to share your own story or give advice! Remember all you learned in Chapter 10: Listen Well. Err on the side of listening versus talking about yourself. Listening is the relational clout that buys trust and acceptance of what you have to share.

Watch out for comparative grief! Try not to relive your similar experience at their expense. This is hard to do because our natural inclination is to make a comparison as a way to express empathy, but this can quickly turn into hijacking their trial and making it about yours. If you focus on listening, you will be less likely to make this mistake.

4. Ask.

Different trials warrant different responses. Asking first allows you to be sure you don't share when it's unwelcome. If what you want to share is time-sensitive advice related to logistics or practicalities, ask before sharing your recommendations.

In the case of illness/diagnosis where you have direct or similar experience, ask if they are looking for counsel as to treatment, expectations, or doctor recommendations. If they are open and want your advice, then you have the green light. Be careful not to overwhelm with information or they might miss the most important considerations. You can always offer and then let them contact you when they are ready.

In the case of divorce, abuse, addiction, helping aging parents, struggles with a child, or other such personal trials, definitely ask before giving advice or sharing your own journey (After lots of listening!). In such situations, one way to come alongside is to keep your sharing in first person, which minimizes the opportunity for the other person to feel judged and makes advice easier to receive.

Proceed with Caution

Keep your motivations in check so you're sharing to encourage—not to be considered the expert or to process your own emotions. Pray diligently, asking for wisdom and discernment.

If you aren't sure whether to share your related story, make a casual reference to your situation in conversation. If the person follows up by asking you a question about your experience, then proceed cautiously. If the first answer leads to another question, then it's likely they want to hear. If not, let it go.

> *Keep your motivations in check so you're sharing to encourage—not to be considered the expert or to process your own emotions.*

You may have planted a seed for later. If and when they are ready, they may seek you out for more information. Don't push if they seem to close down when you open the door. But do be willing to try again another time if you're feeling led.

Using open-ended questions allows plenty of opportunity for them to ask for what they need. Using this technique, you won't unwittingly divert the conversation to your own story or advice if they don't want to hear it.

If you are called to share your experience keep these tips in mind:

- ✓ Show your vulnerability.
- ✓ Be brief.
- ✓ Don't minimize their situation.
- ✓ Don't one-up them.
- ✓ Validate their feelings.
- ✓ Keep your heart motivations in check.
- ✓ Provide only information with direct correlation.
- ✓ Keep it first person. ("Here's what happened to me" or "This was my experience")

We must be willing to open our mouths when God asks, but we must also know when to keep them closed. I hope what we've discussed in this chapter will equip you when and if you're called upon to encourage another because you've been there before.

Chapter 24

when someone is aging

*Honor your father and your mother, as the Lord your God has
commanded you, so that you may live long and that it may go
well with you in the land the Lord your God is giving you.*
–Deuteronomy 5:16 NIV

m y dear mother, Catherine, is 88 years old. She has loved her family of 14 children, our spouses, 38 grandchildren, and eight great-grandchildren well. She has endured more hardship than I will ever comprehend—including single parenting for many years after her divorce from my alcoholic father when I was five years old.

Even through the depths of loss—houses, possessions, marriage, and even a son—she remains a beacon of strength for all her offspring.

And no matter her circumstance, she has always been a living testimony of loving her neighbor.

As a young girl, I often perched atop the counter and watched Mom stir enough ingredients to cover an entire kitchen into her mammoth silver mixing bowl. No fancy Kitchen Aid mixer for her. Two aging cookie sheets, the scratched and worn bowl, a giant metal spoon, and her love were all the tools she needed.

I marveled at how she made the stirring look effortless. Even with her arthritic hands, she wielded the chocolate chip cookie dough—made to five times the original recipe—in a way I never could, no matter how hard I tried. I usually begged for a chance to stir the flour into the creamed butter and sugars, and although it took more time with me at the helm, she allowed it. But I tired quickly under the weight of that beast.

When each batch of cookies was done baking, she would line them up like army troops ready for battle on the wooden chopping block stationed in the center our kitchen. My young, greedy eyes envisioned destroying the whole mound of sweet, chewy goodness. Until the command would come.

"Sarah, can you bag up the cookies in batches of 12?"

My hopes of hoarding all the plunder were quickly dashed as the multitudes dwindled by my own hand.

Decades later, with kids of my own underfoot, I discovered the true nature of what I misattributed to her torturous ways. My mother didn't have much, but she knew how to love others well. Chocolate chip cookies were but one of her weapons.

My mother lived in a way I believe is lacking in my generation—loving others by sharing whatever she had. She shared Christmas fudge, her Sunday dinner table, and homemade treasures of all kinds—from pinecone wreaths to burgeoning bouquets from her cherished flower gardens to piles of quilts stitched together with her own stiffened, aging hands.

She continues to love her neighbor, whether that "neighbor" is her family, an infirm person across the street, or any one of the multitude of friends she quilts, plays bridge, or lunches out with. Her keen eye for the person in need has brought her to many a doorstep with soup, a meal, baked goods, or a helping hand—even when her own hands don't work as well as they once did.

She's shown me there is always enough to give away, no matter how little you have.

A New Reality

My mom was 42 when I was born—her 14th child. So her nest has only been empty for around 25 years, which isn't that long considering her age. She has also provided a soft place for many of her adult children to land at various times and trials of their lives, further demonstrating her generous spirit.

However, now that she is approaching 90, she is finding herself in a new role. A receiving one. The challenging thing about coming alongside someone who's aging, whether you're the child, grandchild, or spouse, is accepting this change. The one who once took care of you or made decisions with you is now asking for advice or looking to you for financial help. And now your job is to lead the way instead of follow.

No matter the person's age, it can be hard to adjust to this new reality. And there will be inevitable challenges as you begin to shift toward caring for someone you love who cannot do what they once could.

Abilities Change

Once vibrant and invincible, we will all become vulnerable and fragile. Anne from Texas said it well. "I always think of my parents like they're in their forties or fifties, but I'm finally realizing they are over seventy and can't do what they once could."

Whenever the revelation happens for you, at some point you will begin to see a shift in a person's energy—and it might rock your world. The notion of your parent or spouse's mortality often follows thereafter. Many aren't ready to face this new awakening. When caring for someone who is aging, it's important to understand this shift in ability isn't only challenging for you—it's life-changing for them as well.

Many of the things we talked about in this book apply to caring for your aging parents or spouse—or to a friend who is coming alongside their aging parents or spouse. Whether the person you love is living on their own, has a spouse (or you are the spouse!) to help care for them, or resides in a nursing or assisted living environment, consider the following ways to come alongside and love them through this new stage of life.

Respect their "new normal."
As my mom has aged, she can no longer stand for long periods of time. She can't lift her arm above her shoulder. She can't turn her head all the way to one side. She can't hear well without her hearing aids. She can't grasp things between her twisted, arthritic fingers. The tasks I'm able to complete effortlessly take her double, or triple, the time, if she can accomplish them at all. Yet she continues to live a vibrant, meaningful, independent life—despite her physical challenges.

I've experienced frustration when I've been incapacitated for extended periods of time, like after back surgery, and found myself unable to accomplish basic daily tasks. My inability was short-lived, but my Mom's is intense and prolonged. I can only imagine how much deeper the frustration!

And her needs are ever changing. We've done little things to help her, like switch to lighter dishes and glasses so she can put them away or keep things on the counter since she can't reach up to the cupboard anymore. We've done bigger things like giving her rides so she doesn't have to drive at night or changing her bathroom and bedroom amenities to suit her new normal.

My mom is quite self-sufficient for her age. Perhaps your parent or spouse's situation is far more intense. But whatever the circumstance, health or otherwise, empathize with deficiencies instead of becoming frustrated or angered by them. It is far harder for them to adjust to a new normal than it is for you!

Realize that even if the aging person is still well enough to be "on their own" or even if they reside in an assisted living or other facility, much of their life still falls to you to help with. Work this into your schedule so that each need isn't an "interruption" but part of *your* new normal. Then if they don't need you for some reason on any given day, you get some extra time for other things.

Be mindful of simple ways you can continue to give them independence and honor their need to feel a part of their own life. If you've ever faced a situation out of your own control, you understand how paralyzing it feels. Allowing the one who is aging to make decisions, perform tasks, and continue activities whenever possible will improve their long-term well being.

Provide practical help.
Just before my mom's 88th birthday, she requested a "monthly helper chart" so she could get the help she needed without the hassle of trying to find someone in each moment. She sent a letter to our entire family asking each of us to be responsible for any help/errands/projects/driving she might need in our allotted month. Now she doesn't have to feel bad for asking because we all know who is "on duty" that month. If the person in charge can't accomplish a certain task, they help her find someone who can.

I love that Mom took ownership of her needs this way. As we talked about in instances of illness or other trials, taking people up on generic offers of "let me know what I can do" can be daunting, especially if the needs have no end date. It feels debilitating when day after day you're incapable of doing what were once routine chores or tasks.

If you offer practical help to an aging parent or other relative—on a schedule or periodically—you will provide much more than the task you complete. You will give them peace of mind and relieve their anxiety about getting things done, which is a great gift in and of itself.

Listen.

It's no secret that when your parent starts to need you more you are often in the busiest "season" of your own life, possibly with a family and career of your own to manage. This can be a difficult "row to hoe," considering your own crops need tending and watering at the same time your parent's field needs maintenance. It can be a tough balancing act, trying to keep the combine churning and yourself on solid ground.

An often-overlooked way we can come alongside our aging parent is by listening to them. As their life slows down, they are more prone to talk about things you might deem trivial, like health concerns or even health concerns of their friends. No matter, listen up!

My friend Pam's mom has been a widow for 28 years. I have always been impressed by her dedication and how she consistently honors her mother in tangible ways, not the least of which is "listening" to her on a regular basis:

> As a kid, I remember lying in my bed listening to my parents when they went to bed at night. There were five kids in the house, so bedtime was their time to talk about whatever needed to be talked about—not to mention their only time alone. When my dad died, I thought it might be important for me to

give that conversation time to my mom, albeit over the phone instead of snuggling next to her. It has been our practice to chat on the phone every night for 28 years. We haven't missed many nights. I usually call her. That's part of the blessing for her—looking forward to the phone ringing when it is dark and late and quiet and hearing someone on the other end who loves her and wants to make sure she is home and safe.

She actually does most of the talking, sometimes repeating the same thing a couple of times, but that's okay. The idea is to give her someone to talk to. My siblings are good about calling her as well. These days, I try to call more than once per day, especially in winter, since she is increasingly home alone. I usually hear the same things both times I call, but that's okay because some day she won't be around for me to call anymore. I am grateful for the opportunity to love on my mom in this way.

Listening is a way to demonstrate great love and support. Value their conversation, engage whenever possible, and give your undivided attention as they share whatever their heart desires.

Keep remembering.
The aging person in your life might face hardship for a month or for decades. That's what makes this particular "trial" harder than others. Although each person's situation is unique, it can be easy to lose sight of this need if the situation continues for years. Don't forget they still need you, even though their daily trials become like background noise amidst the soundtrack of your full life.

As we discussed earlier, it's important you continue to "remember."

Remembering is also important if you're walking alongside a friend who has an aging parent. Be especially mindful of friends who are the only caregivers for those who are aging—with no siblings or children, or whose siblings or children are too far away to help. Reach out to them periodically with text, call, or card to let them know you care. Take a caregiver out regularly if they are in the midst of an acute time so they can get a break and receive some support, too.

Tap into your talents.

Pam and her four siblings each play a role in her mom's care. One sister serves as handyman. One brother stays for long weekends and helps with bigger projects. Another brother is the finance manager and chief advice giver. Another sister is the personal care go-to gal for things like toenail clipping or setting hair in curlers. And Pam goes to her mom's house weekly to help with a full variety of household tasks.

My siblings and I care for our mom similarly. Granted, we have 13 to draw from, but each uses his or her own "talent" as a way to help meet Mom's needs. Consider what you're good at, what you can make time for, and offer this regularly to your parent.

Maintain unity.

David from Texas, who also has aging parents, spoke these wise words: "I think sometimes it's harder dealing with the 'children' of aging parents as they don't always see issues with one mind." To love your parent(s) well it's important to understand the adverse affects of sibling disagreement and competing opinions—especially in front of your parent(s).

If you keep the end game in mind—it's not about you—you can honor your parents by working in a cooperative, not combative, spirit with your siblings.

Be there.

When my dad was still alive, he lived in a nursing home in the same city as my sister Nora and my brother John. In those days, they and their spouses were the chief caretakers for my dad. They loved him well—

showing up with their kids, having him over, taking him to dinner, or meeting him at church. Despite growing families of their own, they always made time to be present with him. This demonstration of love was essential to my dad, who was an extremely social person! I know my dad valued their sacrifice of time to be with him more than most anything else they did for him.

Likewise, Pam makes her mom a priority, dedicating one day a week to go to her house. She does practical things, like filling medications and pill boxes, making doctor appointments and driving her mom to them, tending to the mail, stocking healthy food, and doing household chores. Pam said,

> Sometimes we bake or put jigsaw puzzles together. When she knows I am coming, she washes her sheets so I can help her make the bed. She always jokes how odd it is that every time I come there are clean sheets in the dryer. It is always the same old joke, but isn't predictability and doing the ordinary one of the best parts about coming home to your mom? We usually go out to lunch because that is a treat to her, and too often it involves ice cream for dessert, but I make the sacrifice and choke it down. I scratch her back or give her hugs and kisses so she gets that loving touch. At the end of the day, she stands at the door and waves good-bye and still tells me to buckle up and drive safely. Once a mom, always a mom.

Honoring your mother, father, or spouse is a privilege, not an obligation. Coming alongside as they age will often require putting them first—above your own agenda. But if you desire to honor

Honoring your mother, father, or spouse is a privilege, not an obligation.

them for all the sacrifices they have made for you over the years, you can help those who are aging to live out their days with peace, dignity, love, and joy.

Chapter 25

"messy" situations

For we are his workmanship, created in Christ
Jesus for good works, which God prepared
beforehand, that we should walk in them.
–Ephesians 2:10 ESV

i 've been staying at a shelter. I'm afraid to go home. The person running the shelter said I should call my pastor, and you're the closest thing I've got. Can you help me?"

When I heard those words I wished I hadn't answered my phone. I sat at my desk watching sunlight pouring in my window, the dust dancing in its rays without a care in the world, and all I could think was *why me?* Why was God asking me to foray into this messy, dark place beside a woman I hardly knew?

There wasn't much time to debate God's call—or the one on the other end of the phone line. I agreed to help. Within a few short hours, my new reality included words like abuse, police, court, lawyers, shelters, homelessness, custody, and joblessness. These all came wrapped in the package of a desperate woman with nowhere else to turn—not even her own family.

There were times people told me I shouldn't help her. They said things like, "You don't know what you're getting yourself into," or "Get out as fast as you can."

I won't pretend for one minute it was easy to come alongside someone facing such dire circumstances. It wasn't. But with the help of God and countless others over the course of the next year, we helped this woman get another chance at life.

Today, she has her own townhome, an amazing job, partial custody of her kids, and a vibrant faith in the God who never gave up on her—even when she thought everyone else had.

Many people would run from a situation like this. And believe me, I wanted to. But the reason I said yes wasn't because I'm this great selfless person, it's because I never want to say no to God when he's asks me to love my neighbor—even if it *is* really, really messy.

It Isn't Always Easy

Life isn't only filled with comprehendible situations, such as your best friend's grandma dying at the age of 95. It's also filled with complicated stuff that's hard for people to talk about, much less walk into. In the Grandma-lived-a-long-life death scenario, folks are more apt to know what to do. Cards, condolences, food are all easier actions to take. If the reason for the trial is more delicate—or messy—people are more apt to stay away.

Whether I walked in willingly or not, I've helped through hardships I wish I'd never seen. Alcoholism, suicide, abuse, death of a young child, mental illness, depression, addictions of all kinds, divorce, and teenage struggles, just to name a few. But here's the thing about "messy situations": these neighbors need us to walk alongside them even more! If we want to love our neighbor, as God commands, we will have to leave safe, comfortable, predictable trials (and lives) and venture into unknown waters of messiness.

Because "messy" trials are less socially acceptable, our neighbors who face them are about as lonely as they get. Of course, I'm talking in generalities, but the world tends to be more accepting of those with cancer, illness, or a terminal diagnosis because they don't believe

> *Because "messy" trials are less socially acceptable, our neighbors who face them are about as lonely as they get.*

you did anything to deserve them. And likely, you didn't.

But in life's messiest trials, many people think—and act—differently. They tend to place blame.

> Divorce: "You should have tried harder."
> Suicide: "They aren't going to heaven because they sinned against God."
> Addiction: "If they loved you, they would quit."
> Abuse: "You should just leave."
> Teenage Trials: "You can just make them stop; you're the parent."

People's theology and behavior can defy God's greater laws of redemption and grace. Sadly, we can forget our own human weakness as we focus on someone else's. God's word says, "For all have sinned and fall short of the glory of God." (Romans 3:23 ESV) and "God shows his love for us in that while we were still sinners, Christ died for us." (Romans 5:8 ESV)

I don't see any special exclusions in those verses. I see a God who knows our sinful nature and loves us anyway. I see a God who allows all of us to come under the covering of His sacrifice—His life for ours. I see amazing grace, abounding forgiveness, and buckets of love.

Jesus said to love God and love our neighbor. Even in messy situations.

Messy situations demand grace.

The absence of judgment.

The intangible presence of unconditional love.

And they beg for people brave enough to enter in and walk alongside—to bring hope and light in a dark place where many refuse to tread.

Every chapter we've covered so far has shown you the way. You might need to step more lightly in a delicate trial, but the actions are the same. And there are also a few special instructions I'd like to share in order to help you be as prepared as possible.

Pace Yourself

If a friend is in the midst of a messy situation that includes court, custody, divorce, or any manner of legal proceeding, it's critical you know these things don't move quickly. For many people facing these types of hardship, they can drag out for *years*. In the case of my friend, it was well over a year before she got resolution in her custody situation. Other friends are going on three or four years of challenging legal proceedings.

As someone who's coming alongside, you will need to recognize this could take lots of time to sort out and pace yourself accordingly. If you operate on overdrive, you will quickly tire and not be worth much to your friend for the duration of her trial. There certainly is an acute beginning, but as the situation wears on, it will become more chronic and you will need to establish a manageable pace for serving.

Set Boundaries

Circumstances such as abuse, addiction, divorce, wayward children (of all ages), or custody battles can be all-consuming. There is also a tendency toward desperation, isolation, depression, or frustration, which further compounds the intense needs you might encounter. There likely won't be people lining the halls to help, either, so when and if you are willing to come alongside, the person in trial will be ready for you.

This warning is not meant to keep you away but to give you an understanding before you begin that you need to have clear boundaries in place so you aren't giving or doing more than you can handle. If you set your limits early, you'll avoid losing a friend over feeling taken advantage of or because you fell prey to the exhaustion of over-helping. We don't want that.

The woman I mentioned in the opening of this chapter literally had nothing when she called me. My initial instinct was to do everything for her. But my wise husband helped me set safe parameters from the beginning. I gave lots of my time, and even some money, but we drew the line at giving her a place to live in our house. It was hard for me not to offer when she desperately needed a place to stay, but I knew I had to keep my own family life stable as well as maintain my own sanity and peace in order to continue helping her.

We focused on four areas of involvement in her situation—finding her a place to live, a job, a car, and fair legal representation so she would have a chance to keep her children. We shared the load whenever possible, and amazing Christian sisters collaborated beautifully to support this woman. Help came in many forms: care packages, bedding and air mattresses, furniture, a temporary basement bedroom, a loan for a down payment on a car, job leads, childcare, Christmas presents, legal fees, moving assistance, and the first month's rent for a new townhome.

The end result of our help turned out well. Of course, that's not always the case. But if you go into the situation with your eyes open, seeking God faithfully for His guidance, trusting Him for strength, and willing to be obedient and loving, you will always be doing the right thing, even if the outcome isn't what you'd hoped for.

It can be harder to muster the courage to walk alongside a friend in a messy trial more than others. Folks don't often line up to bring the casserole when they're afraid of what's behind the closed door. But if you step out in faith to love these neighbors, you'll know you've been used as God's instrument in a way not many others are willing to attempt.

And I can testify: obeying Him by blessing a friend in deep despair will bring some of life's greatest rewards.

Chapter 26

terminal illness

By this all people will know that you are my
disciples, if you have love for one another.
–John 13:35 ESV

t appeared to be an ordinary day as I chatted easily on the phone with my older sister Terry. But if you looked for more than a moment, you couldn't miss the harsh reality we were living. Our dear brother-in-law Tom was in the last few weeks of his battle with melanoma.

We were discussing how some people "just know what to do" in these situations and how others lack the understanding to be helpful. And then big sister asked littlest sister, "How can I help? I'm not sure what I should do."

Let me be clear, Terry was already *really good* at loving others in their hard circumstances. I had seen her do it more times than I could count! But this was different; she hadn't been *this* close to terminal illness before now. Unfortunately, I had. Twice. Before I knew it, I was sharing information I didn't know I had. Or maybe it was information I just hadn't put it into words before that day.

About a year later, I decided I had no choice but to write this book. I concluded there must be more people who want to help and don't know the most effective way. That, and the perseverance, faith, and strength of Kelley, Deborah, and Tom, who each graciously allowed me to be part of their end-of-life journey, provided even more incentive.

Caution: Acute Situation Ahead

I am not an expert, but I have learned a thing or two in the trenches of terminal illness. My prayer is you'd not only be willing to come alongside in that difficult time, but also that you'd go forth with an abundance of courage, grace, and love.

The following advice is appropriate for Tier 1 or 2 relationships, although if you have personal experience in this area and are Tier 3 or 4 you may be called upon to help. The areas I've decided to focus on in this chapter are unique to terminal illness, but all of the actions we've covered thus far apply. Hopefully this advice will give you insight if you've not traveled the road of terminal illness before.

Go gingerly.

During his time as primary caregiver for our terminally ill friend Deborah, Gary said he got so tired of hearing, "How's Deborah doing?" He told me, "I wanted to say 'Are you kidding me? How's she doing? She's dying!' And their follow up would always be, "How are you doing, Gary?" I would want to respond 'I'm watching the woman who stole my heart die. How do you think I'm doing?'"

When there are no words, let there be no words.

We mean to be empathetic. We mean to be caring. But in the face of terminal illness, there's not much to say. So as you go into it, remember, it's delicate. When there are no words, let there be no words.

If you have experience with terminal illness, you will be a valuable asset with instant credibility. Even so, it's important to understand it's not you facing death. You might be able to share more personally than a different third party, but you still need to be full of grace. Try not to speak in "you shoulds" but instead say, "you might need to consider" or "this is what you might expect to happen" or "this is what I experienced."

You never want to compare if the comparison isn't helpful. Be sure you are focused on the person, not yourself—it's not about you—and ask permission before sharing advice whenever possible.

Be present.

In the case of terminal illness, being present is more essential than ever.

Jenny, a hospice and home care nurse for several years, admits to facing frustration when she wasn't able to fix people's situation and didn't have perfect words to make it better for those families in her care. But she's learning along the way. "My patients and their families have taught me they aren't looking for magic advice or solutions from me—or anyone for that matter. They just want people to be present. To show they care."

Additionally, if you're a welcomed presence, you can be a gatekeeper of sorts—acting as a filter so the person or family doesn't have to interact with too many people when their energy is waning.

Be willing to take the heat.

When Tom was in his final days, my sister and her boys wanted those precious moments with him. We have a large family, and Tom and Mary have a huge network of friends, so you can imagine how many people wanted the chance to be there. They were never short of offers of help, but in the end, it was about Tom, my sister, and her boys, not everyone else.

Since I didn't live nearby, I traveled to their home for a week to be available if Mary needed me, but I stayed elsewhere. I offered to come by each day, but waited to see if she wanted me. I ended up at their house every day for five days.

I tried to be present but not intrusive. I made myself scarce but available if she needed to rest, go out, or just walk to the mailbox. I was close if she wanted to talk, silent if she didn't. I offered prayer at least once each day. I sat with Tom when needed but stayed away if family or another friend wanted to be there instead.

It got a little harder when Mary wanted me to be there but didn't always want other people. The family needed calm and quiet—and fewer visitors. I had to be willing to take the heat from those who wondered why they weren't allowed in.

Choose your battles.

It's life and death, so the trivial stuff—like cleaning out the refrigerator—pales in comparison. Follow the lead of the person facing terminal illness or those close to him. Your normal agenda doesn't apply, and you will need to choose wisely.

Not long ago, a group of my treasured Bible study friends stepped in to help a friend who had been given a terminal diagnosis. They each used their unique gifts—decorating, accounting, organizing, planning, compassion, to bless this friend, just as described in Chapter 18: Tap into

Your Talents and Chapter 19: Collaborate. One woman even offered to let the patient move into her home!

As the group planned out the patient's new room, there were several opinions that differed from the woman with the terminal diagnosis. For the sake of aesthetics and practicality, the women were trying to talk their friend out of something she really wanted. I gently reminded them how it must feel for someone facing death to have to let go of even a few of her treasured things.

In the end, these women jumped through hoops to be sure their friend got what she had wanted to begin with, despite their personal opinions on the subject. I am so proud they loved our friend the way she needed to be loved, and didn't dig their heels in about something unimportant.

Proceed as normal.
One day my husband, Craig, and I were scheduled to attend a basketball game with Kelley and her husband, Randy. Earlier the same day Kelley found out her leukemia had returned. We offered to cancel, thinking they would want to stay home and process the news. But they wanted to keep life as normal as possible and proceed with our plans. I remember one of them saying, "We can't just sit at home and look at each other and talk about dying again."

Death was their daily reality.

As a rule, I tried to be very discerning about when and how often I brought up her illness. That night, we were left to decide whether to talk about the elephant in the room or not. Craig and I decided since it was so raw and new that we had to address it somehow, but we didn't want to make it the night's focus. When we met to head out to the game, we asked if we could pray over them before we left. They agreed. We continued on with as normal a night as possible when you learn that your best friend's cancer has returned. I don't think we watched much basketball that night, but we didn't talk about dying either.

This advice is definitely easier said than done, but do your best to honor what normalcy you can.

Help them "give away."

One part of loving someone in their last days on earth involves being available to help them "give away" what they need to give away. I don't mean only tangible items, although that can be the case, too. I'm referring to the intangibles of one's life—details, directives, emotions, feelings, apologies.

We have an innate need to tie up loose ends. Imagine how you feel as you leave the house on an extended trip. Now multiply that feeling by 1,000. Your job alongside someone with a terminal illness, if you're willing to accept it, is to give them a safe place to express what they need to say. As a general rule, listen more than you speak.

There is something powerful and sacred about "dying words." Don't drown them out with your own, unless asked for your advice or opinion. There will be time to process your feelings after they're gone, and God will be with you in the tears and questions.

Offer specific help.

We've talked throughout the book about countless ways to be of help, some of which depend on the depth of your relationship with the person. Assuming you're as close to someone as I became with Deborah, you can help with more sensitive items. Because I had experience, I helped her plan her funeral and write her obituary. I also helped by typing letters to her boys that she dictated to me. And we made a list of what items she wanted to give away to whom.

In Kelley's case, though very sick and in the hospital, she wasn't in hospice per se. Several of us helped with scrapbooks for her children, because that was a top priority for her. There were times she said little things to me about her children that she wanted me to know. I listened and catalogued, knowing those memories were part of what she needed to give to someone else.

In my sister Mary's case, I offered to help write a Caring Bridge entry for Tom's site when she didn't have the energy during the last weeks of his life. She later told me it helped her immensely because she simply had no emotional margin in which to write it, despite the necessity to communicate to others what was going on. By using what I had written as a base, she read it and decided what to add, change or delete instead of having to start from scratch.

There are many practical yet intimate ways you can offer to help either the patient or their family. You can offer to help with obituaries, funeral arrangements, programs, cemetery plots, photo boards, videos, general inquiries, flowers, or clothes shopping. If you have personal experience in losing a loved one, you might have more options based on what you found helpful.

Always be sensitive to the person's openness before you ask certain questions and never pressure them to receive help or give answers. Some details will not be as high on their list of priorities as they might be on yours. Remember, it's not about you.

Always be sensitive to the person's openness before you ask certain questions and never pressure them to receive help or give answers.

Phrase specific offers to give them a choice whether to accept your help or not.

- "I can come along if you want to choose a dress for the funeral or help you get clothes for your kids."
- "What can I help you with that you don't have energy to do?"

- "I have experience writing obituaries. Would you like me to get you started?"
- "Would you like my help writing a Caring Bridge entry?"
- "What calls I can make for you?"
- "What errands can I do for you?"

Give them control whenever possible.

I cannot imagine for a moment what it must be like to be the person in a hospice situation. My gut tells me it would be frustrating to know that no matter what you do or don't do, you can't change the outcome of your life. I've seen it up close, but I still don't pretend to fully comprehend the struggle.

I do think, though, that while someone is coherent and alert, we can find ways to be helpful without making them feel incapable. Even if you can do a task faster and easier alone, put your agenda aside to honor their need to be able to do something for themselves. When your very life is out of your control, it's a small pleasure to do something for yourself.

Come alongside instead of stripping them of their independence.

Let their no be no.

We're all human. And all this selfless loving our neighbor can get hard when someone you love is reaching the end of her life. We want to say goodbye, make our peace, say what they mean to us. But sometimes that's not what the terminally ill person or their family needs from you. Each situation is different, but I learned this one the hard way.

I didn't know it at the time, but the last email I would send to Kelley was a request for a brief visit. She wasn't speaking at that point—she'd had a tracheotomy in place for over a week. We communicated by email between visits, or if in person, she wrote on a white board. I had the feeling she didn't want me to come, but I pressed for clarification.

She replied, "It was actually a no, but maybe you could come by for 30 minutes or so."

I wrote back. "It's ok. You need to let your no be no. I can come another time."

I had an intuition that night I would never see her again this side of heaven. It was excruciating. But somehow I knew that moment wasn't about me. It was about her, her family, her children, her husband—not one of her closest friends, as much as it pained me. I knew God wanted me to stay home, but I was profoundly sad about it. So I invited a friend over and we prayed.

Kelley passed away the next morning, surrounded by her family.

Would I have loved to see her just one more time? Of course! But I needed to honor her request and her needs above all else, even when it was the hardest thing I've ever done.

Pray.

When my brother-in-law Tom was facing terminal Melanoma, I felt very convicted by God to pray over him whenever I could, probably because of the profound effect it had in my life when others did the same for me. At the time, it was difficult for Tom and Mary to attend church often because it was overwhelming to face everyone—the questions, the conversations, and the hard reality of terminal illness. So I felt even more called to provide spiritual encouragement in the form of prayer, especially for Tom, in this critical time.

Tom was always like a big brother to me, and we had a sweet relationship even though I didn't live nearby. Many of our family and friends felt the same about him. It didn't matter how long it had been since you had last seen him, Tom always made you feel special and cherished in his presence.

On one occasion during his illness, my husband and I planned a weekend road trip with him and my sister to see our beloved Wisconsin

Badger football team play in the Big 10 Conference Championship. After an awesome victory and two precious days together, I felt a strong prompting to pray with Tom before we left. I couldn't put it off because I wasn't sure when we'd see him again. As we walked into the house I was sweating, thinking *you're not leaving until you've prayed with him.*

It's not that I believed Tom wouldn't be open to my prayers, but we'd never prayed together before. Don't imagine I am some super pray-er, praying all the time. Even in this area I believe to be so important, it can still be hard for me to summon the courage to pray with people, even when I feel led. But then I think back to my friend Pam who was brave enough to pray over me, and I get over my self-doubt. Her leap of faith changed my life considerably, so I know it's worth any inherent risk to my self-esteem.

I often ask myself, "What is the worst thing that could happen?" They might say no, but I believe my God is big enough to make a way. And even if they refuse, I can handle a little rejection in the name of bringing the power of prayer to someone I love! (By the way, no one has ever rejected my offer to pray.)

Finally, after the bags were loaded, goodbyes and hugs complete, I mustered the courage. "Tom, before we leave would you mind if we pray over you?"

He replied without a moment's pause. "I would love that."

There in the living room, five of us circled around him in prayer. Any risk I felt beforehand was worth the overwhelming joy of standing in the gap for someone I loved in his time of trial. After all, God says, "Do not be anxious about anything, but in every situation, by prayer and petition, with thanksgiving, present your requests to God." (Philippians 4:6 NIV)

That day opened the door for me to offer prayer each time I saw Tom in person throughout his illness. Because we shared relationship, respect, and trust, we had the blessing of sweet times of prayer. I sensed God's confirmation that it was chief among my purposes during the few times I could visit.

As Tom's life drew near its end, I made that special visit where I had the privilege of seeing him every day for five days. On my first day there, he was failing physically but still quite lucid. I offered to pray, as had become our custom.

"Your prayers are always welcome. I love it when you pray," he said.

I'd never heard sweeter words! I was so moved by God's faithfulness in allowing me to bring Tom comfort of any kind. I quickly said, "Then I promise to pray with you every day I'm here this week."

Friends, as a life draws to a close it can be heartbreaking, but it is sacred. God gives, and He takes away. In that precious week with my sister and her husband, we had many times of prayer with the whole family as well as privately with only Tom and me.

The day Tom spoke for the last time, I was sitting with him, ready to say my final goodbye before I left. His hospital bed was in the dining room on the main floor. While he rested, streams of light washed over him as the late afternoon sun found its way through the trees into our precious space. I was compelled to remind him of God's promises and assurance. I sat for a few minutes praying silently. I felt God's presence with us.

When I was able, I asked him through my tears, "Tom do you know you're forgiven and loved by God? Do you know that no matter what you've done—or left undone—He's waiting to accept you into Heaven with loving arms?"

Words were a struggle by then, but his faint reply was clear. "I do."

"And do you accept God's gift of grace to you, knowing he died for you?"

"I do."

Then I offered one last prayer over him. I don't remember any of the words, just the essence. The Spirit interceded on my behalf and gave me words to pray.

Days later, Mary requested prayer by telephone from my sister Terry and me, who were away on a pre-planned trip with our families. "It meant a lot when you shared the burden with us through prayer. You helped us say what we couldn't say ourselves at the time," Mary later told me. That sacred moment happened within hours of the end of Tom's life—us on our knees in a room in Florida praying over a speakerphone, she, Tom, and her boys in a room in Wisconsin.

The beauty of prayer is that it provides a means for you to speak on your loved one's behalf, to share the burden, to lift them before the throne of God. It can be an opportunity to provide assurance, as in the case of Tom, or a chance to speak about salvation to someone you love. No matter the situation, it's always a holy opportunity and privilege to stand in the gap for someone, especially in the end of life.

You don't need perfect words, only a willing heart. God will provide the rest.

conclusion

Arise, for it is your task, and we are with you; be strong and do it.
–Ezra 10:4 ESV

I 've learned that the hardest things in life are those most worth doing—whether it's doing what others won't do, what you are gifted to do, or what you're feeling called by God to do. There's a big, broken world out there waiting for your neighborly love.

The pages of this book were written to equip you. To encourage you. To embolden you to come alongside your neighbors in the face of their trial. They weren't written for information only, they were written to incite action. In the Bible, James writes, "Faith by itself isn't enough. Unless it produces good deeds, it is dead and useless." (James 2:17 NLT)

You now hold the answer to the complicated question, "What can I do to help?" And you have the tools you need to follow through. From now on, when you see those in trial around you, you will be faced with a choice—to follow God's command to love your neighbor or to stay within the confines of your own comfort. My prayer is for you to walk across the street, yard, sanctuary, hallway, or office—wherever God's calling—and be bold, brave, and generous with your love.

I promise, the journey is worth every minute. And as you step out in faith to love your neighbor, no matter the trial, know that I'm cheering for you!

And God will be right there, too . . . alongside.

acknowledgements

For over two decades, I dreamed of writing a book. Of course, in my dreams there were long lines of fans waiting inside a legit bookstore for my signature on the pages of my New York Times Bestseller. But as misguided and self-centered as that notion was, I was also wrong about something else: I never imagined my first book would be about this topic. Proof positive that God's plans are bigger than all our misconceptions, misguided motivations, and self-aggrandizing strivings.

Thankfully, He reshaped my dream. He used trial to bring purpose. He used ashes to bring beauty. He used challenges to bring insight. And he allowed me to grow in my longing to help as many people as possible become better at loving their neighbor through trial.

Through the painstaking and grueling process of the over four years it's taken me to write this book, there were days I never thought I'd get here—to you holding a real, tangible copy of a book (or a tablet that has the electronic words!). But along the way, I was repeatedly convinced of the need for the message in *Alongside*.

And I was encouraged by many faithful friends, family, and fellow sojourners who helped to make my dream of becoming an author a reality:

To Randy Lewis, Gary Stevens, and Mary Dallmann, three people I love—who lost those they loved most. *Alongside* happened in great part because of you. Thank you for being courageous and vulnerable enough to let me share a piece of your story so others can learn from it. Even though I wish the circumstances that prompted your experience had never happened, I am changed because I walked with you through loss. You taught me about selflessness and love in the midst of anguish.

To Kelley Lewis, Deborah Whitaker and Tom Dallmann, who were loved deeply by many. I'm grateful they allowed me into their suffering and into the holiness that came with it.

Kelley, a true sister in Christ, walked with me and lived out her life verse, "Be faithful in prayer, patient in affliction and give thanks in all circumstance." She exemplified grace, patience, courage, humility, kindness, love, peace, and thankfulness. I owe a debt of gratitude for all she taught me that will only be repaid to those I love on this Earth. I look forward to the day when we can "walk" on streets of gold together in Heaven!

Deborah demonstrated beauty and elegance in all things and cared for my children as if they were her own. Her grace was unparalleled, her attention to detail and service to others continue to impact my life.

Tom remained positive no matter the adversity and maintained his "can-do" spirit until the end. His kindness, humility, and perseverance remain an example to all who knew him. Forever he is etched in this Badger-lover's heart, and each time I sing "On Wisconsin," I see his face.

To the soul sisters who listened to me read my early insights over coffee and scones and shared their hardships and insights. Rita, Angie, Lori, Seaneen, Pauline, Mallory, Patricia, Kris—I might never have endeavored this project without your early advice and encouragement years ago in Rita's living room.

To all those who bravely shared their personal stories and sage advice: Gary, Rita, Karen, Pauline, Angie, Kris S., Seaneen, Kay, Kathy, Keith, Michele, Lora, Kris K., Lori, Jenny, Linda, Marijo, Stephanie K., Audrey, Madi, Ben and Susie, Dick, MarthaJoy, Dan, Pam, Allison, Mitch, Susie M., Aileen, Michelle, Julia, Astrid, Tiffany, Erica, Becky, Annabet, Claire, Laura, Holly, Sandra, Jackie, Stephanie P., Gigi and Dave, Anne, David P., Barb F. and Mary. I appreciated every short conversation, text exchange, Facebook interaction, and lengthy interview, but mostly I cherish my relationship with each of you. It wasn't easy to relive past hardships and hurts, and this book is richer for your stories told through its pages.

To Dee, Cassie, Stephanie P., Dawn and Heather, who cheered and supported in so many big and small ways—and tolerated my insufferable ramblings about all things book writing and publishing.

To my dear friend, Keith Ferrin, who spent hours on the phone and via email informing me about publishing! Thank you for cheering on a novice author and answering my unending questions. And for sharing your signature line, so I could have the perfect book title. Your imprint will always be clear.

To the many faithful prayer warriors, so many I can't mention them all by name, but especially Dee Whaley and my Wednesday Morning Bible Study Girls. And to our Sunday Night Bible Study Group, thank you for your steadfast support and faithfulness as the book topped the prayer list week after week!

To beta readers Beth Johnson, Mallory Polk, Lora Peters, Karen Linscott, Lori Friedrichs, Stacy Cholas, Rita Ward, Pam Blake, Kay Mendyke, Blair Ciecko, and Heather Carroll, thank you for your time and talents. Your invaluable comments, wisdom and feedback made this book immeasurably better.

To my first New Mexico friend, Cassie Sanchez, thank you for loving this neighbor when she moved to the desert and had no friends. And I won't soon forget your 10th inning relief when you helped with details, research, and busy work for the book that my brain just couldn't handle.

To Susie Albert Miller, who believed in the message of *Alongside* enough to recommend me to an amazing acquisitions editor in Karen Anderson. Just when I was about to give up, you two women showed me that God had bigger plans for the book. Thank you both for your friendship and dedication to our craft and our Creator.

To the team at Morgan James Publishing, thank you for putting up with this uptight, first-time author and for helping to create a product worthy of someone's bookshelf or nightstand. I appreciate your personal attention, how you honor God, and the value you place on each book that comes across your desks.

To my amazing editor Anne Mateer, who is long-suffering and talented, all wrapped into one phenomenal package. Your attention to detail and your content insights, not to mention your ability to help me correct years of inadvertent poor writing habits, will bless my readers abundantly. And I appreciated the "U-rah-rah this book is great!" feedback when I struggled with self-doubt.

To my treasured friend Michele Cushatt, you inspire me every day. Your gift as a communicator is unparalleled, and I'm blessed by the words you crafted in the Foreward of this book. Despite the reality you've been living, you continue to provide an anchor of hope for so many who traverse dark and stormy seas. Thank you for your grace, courage, honesty, loyalty, wisdom, and encouragement. Your friendship is a precious jewel in my life.

To my mom, Catherine Moran, who at age 88 motivates me every day to press on no matter how hard life gets. And who always loved her family and friends like everyone ought to love their neighbor. I'm so happy you can see my name on the cover of a book that honors the memory of the many pans of chocolate chip cookies, cinnamon rolls, and fudge you gave away as you loved so many folks in your lifetime.

To my delightful teenagers (Yes, delightful!), Nick, Dani, and Mo. I never dreamed how much I'd love being your mom and how proud of you I'd be. Your support each step of the way, your sacrifice of having me around less as I entered a new stage in life as an author, and your pride in my accomplishment bring me to tears. Each expression of "Way to go Mom!" bolstered my resolve to finish so you'd be proud of me. You three rival any other joy I could experience in this lifetime. #proudmom #iknowiembarrassyoubutyouarestuckwithme

To my Barnabus—Craig. Without you, there'd be no book. When I wanted to give up, you held me up. When I said it wasn't good enough, you said it was. When I didn't think I could do it, you told me I could. I am indebted to you for the constant encouragement and for all the big and small ways you helped me to start—and finish—this book. Thank you also for your sacrifice each time God calls me to walk alongside others. I'm grateful that you never grow weary of my complaints, inadequacies, or failings. And that you tirelessly remind me of the grace that saved us and the grace that should be given. Here's to each day God gives us together and to loving our neighbor in every situation.

And finally, to the One who made me perfect in His sight. Thank you for redeeming me and loving me unconditionally. And for walking alongside me every day.

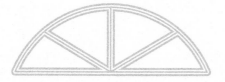

appendix

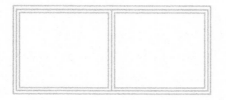

bible verses for loving your neighbor

Trial:

Deuteronomy 31:6 Be strong and courageous. Do not be afraid or terrified because of them, for the Lord your God goes with you; He will never leave or forsake you. Do not be afraid.

Job 11:18–19 You will be secure, because there is hope; you will look about you and take your rest in safety. You will lie down, with no one to make you afraid, and many will court your favor.

Psalm 16:8 I keep my eyes always on the Lord. With Him at my right hand, I will not be shaken.

Psalm 27:1 The Lord is my light and my salvation—whom shall I fear? The Lord is the stronghold of my life—of whom shall I be afraid?

Psalm 121:1–2 I lift up my eyes to the mountains—where does my help come from? My help comes from the Lord, the Maker of heaven and earth.

Isaiah 41:10 So do not fear, for I am with you. Do not be dismayed for I am your God. I will strengthen you and help you. I will uphold you with my righteous hand.

Isaiah 43:2 When you pass through the waters, I will be with you; and when you pass through the rivers, they will not sweep over you. When you walk through the fire, you will not be burned; the flames will not set you ablaze.

Philippians 4:19 And my God will meet all your needs according to the riches of His glory in Christ Jesus.

Hebrews 4:16 Let us then approach God's throne of grace with confidence, so that we may receive mercy and find grace to help us in our time of need.

James 1:2–4 Consider it pure joy, my brothers and sisters, whenever you face trials of many kinds, because you know that the testing of your faith produces perseverance. Let perseverance finish its work so that you may be mature and complete, not lacking anything.

Comfort:

Exodus 14:14 The Lord will fight for you, you need only to be still.

Jeremiah 32:17 Ah, Sovereign LORD, you have made the heavens and the earth by Your great power and outstretched arm. Nothing is too hard for You.

Psalm 46:1 God is our refuge and strength, an ever-present help in trouble.

Psalm 46:10 Be still and know that I am God.

Psalm 91:4 He will cover you with his feathers, and under his wings you will find refuge; his faithfulness will be your shield and rampart.

Matthew 5:4 Blessed are those who mourn, for they will be comforted.

Luke 18:27 What is impossible with man is possible with God.

Ephesians 3:17b–18 And I pray that you, being rooted and established in love, may have power, together with all the Lord's holy people, to grasp how wide and long and high and deep is the love of Christ, and to know this love that surpasses knowledge—that you may be filled to the measure of all the fullness of God.

2 Corinthians 1:3–4 Praise be to the God and Father of our Lord Jesus Christ, the Father of compassion and the God of all comfort, who comforts us in all our troubles, so that we can comfort those in any trouble with the comfort we ourselves receive from God.

Faith:

Lamentations 3:24 I say to myself, "The Lord is my portion; therefore I will wait for Him."

Luke 1:37 For no word from God will ever fail.

Ephesians 3:20–21 Now to Him who is able to do immeasurably more than all we ask or imagine, according to His power that is at work within us, to him be the glory for ever and ever.

1 Corinthians 16:13 Be on your guard; stand firm in the faith; be courageous; be strong.

2 Corinthians 5:7 For we live by faith, not by sight.

James 1:3 Because you know that the testing of your faith produces perseverance.

Hebrews 11:1 Now faith is confidence in what we hope for and assurance about what we do not see.

Grief:

Psalm 9:9 The LORD is a refuge for the oppressed, a stronghold in times of trouble.

Psalm 18:28 You, LORD, keep my lamp burning; my God turns my darkness into light.

Psalm 34:18 The LORD is close to the brokenhearted and saves those who are crushed in spirit.

Psalm 55:22 Cast your cares on the Lord and He will sustain you; He will never let the righteous be shaken.

Ps 59:16 But I will sing of your strength, in the morning I will sing of your love; for you are my fortress, my refuge in time of trouble.

Psalm 126:5 Those who sow in tears, will reap with songs of joy.

Psalm 145:14 The Lord upholds all who fall and lifts up all who are bowed down.

Psalm 147:3 He heals the brokenhearted and binds up their wounds.

Lamentations 3:22–23 Because of the Lord's great love, we are not consumed, for His compassions never fail. They are new every morning; great is Your faithfulness.

Matthew 5:4 Blessed are those who mourn, for they will be comforted.

Revelation 21:4 He will wipe every tear from their eyes. There will be no more death or mourning or crying or pain, for the old order of things has passed away.

Guidance/Protection:

Psalm 18:32 It is God who arms me with strength and keeps my way secure.

Psalm 37:23–24 The Lord makes firm the steps of the one who delights in Him; though he may stumble, he will not fall, for the Lord upholds him with His hand.

Psalm 56:3–4 When I am afraid, I put my trust in you. In God, whose word I praise—in God I trust and am not afraid. What can mere mortals do to me?

Psalm 63:8 I cling to you; Your right hand upholds me.

Psalm 91:11 For He will command his angels concerning you to guard you in all your ways.

Psalm 119:114 You are my refuge and my shield; I have put my hope in Your word.

Isaiah 30:21 Whether you turn to the right or to the left, your ears will hear a voice behind you, saying, "This is the way; walk in it."

Jeremiah 29:11 For I know the plans I have for you," declares the LORD, "plans to prosper you and not to harm you, plans to give you hope and a future.

Hope:

Psalm 31:24 Be strong and take heart, all you who hope in the LORD.

Psalm 62:5–8 Yes, my soul, find rest in God; my hope comes from Him. Truly He is my rock and my salvation; He is my fortress, I will not be shaken. My salvation and my honor depend on God; He is my mighty rock, my refuge. Trust in Him at all times, you people; pour out your hearts to Him, for God is our refuge.

Lamentations 3:25 The Lord is good to those whose hope is in Him, to the one who seeks Him.

Isaiah 61:1b–3 He has sent me to bind up the brokenhearted, to proclaim freedom for the captives and release from darkness for the prisoners, to proclaim the year of the LORD's favor and the day of vengeance of our God, to comfort all who mourn, and provide for those who grieve in Zion—to bestow on them a crown of beauty instead of ashes, the oil of joy instead of mourning, and a garment of praise instead of a spirit of despair. They will be called oaks of righteousness, a planting of the LORD for the display of his splendor.

Romans 5:3–4 Not only so, but we also glory in our sufferings, because we know that suffering produces perseverance; perseverance, character; and character, hope.

Romans 5:5 And hope does not put us to shame, because God's love has been poured out into our hearts through the Holy Spirit, who has been given to us.

Romans 15:13 May the God of hope fill you with all joy and peace as you trust in Him, so that you may overflow with hope by the power of the Holy Spirit.

2 Thessalonians 2:16–17 May our Lord Jesus Christ Himself and God our Father, who loved us and by His grace gave us eternal encouragement and good hope, encourage your hearts and strengthen you in every good deed and word.

Peace:

Psalm 4:8 In peace I will lie down and sleep, for you alone, LORD, make me dwell in safety.

Psalm 29:11 The LORD gives strength to his people; the LORD blesses his people with peace.

Proverbs 3:24 When you lie down, you will not be afraid; when you lie down, your sleep will be sweet.

Isaiah 26:3 You will keep in perfect peace those whose minds are steadfast, because they trust in you.

Isaiah 54:10 Though the mountains be shaken and the hills be removed, yet My unfailing love for you will not be shaken nor My covenant of peace be removed," says the LORD, who has compassion on you.

Matthew 11:28 Come to Me, all you who are weary and burdened, and I will give you rest.

John 14:27 Peace I leave with you; my peace I give you. I do not give to you as the world gives. Do not let your hearts be troubled and do not be afraid.

Philippians 4:6-7 Do not be anxious about anything, but in every situation, by prayer and petition, with thanksgiving, present your requests to God. And the peace of God, which transcends all understanding, will guard your hearts and your minds in Christ Jesus.

2 Thessalonians 3:16 Now may the Lord of peace Himself give you peace at all times and in every way. The Lord be with all of you.

1 Peter 5:7 Cast all your anxiety on Him because He cares for you.

Prayer:

Job 22:27 You will pray to Him, and He will hear you, and you will fulfill your vows.

Jeremiah 29:12 You will call upon Me and come and pray to Me, and I will listen to you.

Matthew 21:22 If you believe, you will receive whatever you ask for in prayer.

John 14:13–14 And I will do whatever you ask in my name, so that the Father may be glorified in the Son. You may ask me for anything in My name, and I will do it.

1 John 5:14 This is the confidence we have in approaching God: that if we ask anything according to His will, He hears us.

websites/books

Support:

CaringBridge–"To amplify the love, hope and compassion in the world, making each health journey easier." This website allows people to easily get updates and offer support and encouragement. (www.caringbridge. org)

CarePages–Free patient blogs and personalized websites that connect friends and family during a health challenge. (www.carepages.com)

HealingWell.com–"Living mindfully and healing well with chronic illness." This website is a support community with blogs, videos, newsletters, articles, and resources to help manage chronic illness. (www. healingwell.com)

Stephen's Ministry–Provides resources and training to improve your ability to relate to and care for others, grow in faith, and journey through life crises. (www.stephenministries.org)

Meal Coordination:

CareCalendar–A web-based calendar that coordinates meals and other care. (www.carecalendar.org)

Take Them a Meal–"Simplifying meal coordination so friends can show they care." (www.takethemameal.com)

Lotsa Helping Hands–"Create a Care Community. Easily organize meals and help for friends and family in need." (www.lotsahelpinghands. com)

Meal Train–"Organized meal giving around significant life events." Interactive, online meal calendar, invitations via e-mail and Facebook, plus an optional donation fund add-on. (www.mealtrain.com)

CaringMeals.com–"A free service that helps you coordinate meals for your friends and family in their time of need." (www.caringmeals.com)

Online Fundraising:

YouCaring–"A free crowdfunding platform that empowers people to help others overcome hardships and enjoy happier, healthier lives." (www.youcaring.com)

GoFundMe–Create your own fundraising campaign to share with family and friends. (www.gofundme.com)

CrowdRise–"Online fundraising for causes you care about." (www. crowdrise.com)

Fundly–Raise Money For Anything. Fundly has no raise requirements. (www.fundly.com)

GiveForward–"GiveForward is the first place to turn when you or someone you love is facing a challenge. From sending a simple 'Thinking of You' to raising money for out-of-pocket expenses, GiveForward empowers anyone to build a community and take action when it counts." (www.giveforward.com)

Faith Gifts/Books

Christian Books (www.cbd.com)
Dayspring (www.dayspring.com)
Lifeway (www.lifeway.com/n/Gifts)
Mary & Martha (www.maryandmartha.com)

Devotional Books

Jesus Calling by Sarah Young—Words of reassurance, comfort, and hope written as if Jesus was speaking to you personally.
Grace for the Moment by Max Lucado—"Reflections to draw you closer to God as well as understand His direction and timing."
Streams in the Desert by Charles Cowman—"Offers wisdom and insight for applying Biblical truths to the ups and downs of everyday life."

Cookbooks

Beating Cancer with Nutrition by Patrick Quillin
Nourish: The Cancer Care Cookbook by Penny Brohn Cancer Care and Christine Bailey

notes

notes

about the author

 Sarah Beckman is a speaker, writer, blogger, and the founder of Salt and clay ministries. Her passion for loving her neighbor has fueled her life and ministry for over ten years, giving her the opportunity to write and speak to audiences across the country. She has a B.A. in Journalism from the University of Wisconsin-Madison and also works as a communications coach and corporate trainer.

Sarah currently lives in Albuquerque, NM with her husband of 24 years, Craig. They have three delightful children ages 15, 17, and 19. Sarah loves spending time with family and friends, golfing, hiking, sailing, entertaining, being still at the lake, leading mission trips to Haiti, and eating green chile.

Connect with Sarah

www.sarahbeckman.org

www.alongsidebook.com

A free eBook edition is available with the purchase of this book.

To claim your free eBook edition:
1. Download the Shelfie app.
2. Write your name in upper case in the box.
3. Use the Shelfie app to submit a photo.
4. Download your eBook to any device.

Shelfie

A free eBook edition is available
with the purchase of this print book.

CLEARLY PRINT YOUR NAME ABOVE IN UPPER CASE

Instructions to claim your free eBook edition:
1. Download the Shelfie app for Android or iOS
2. Write your name in **UPPER CASE** above
3. Use the Shelfie app to submit a photo
4. Download your eBook to any device

Print & Digital Together Forever.

Snap a photo

Free eBook

Read anywhere

CPSIA information can be obtained
at www.ICGtesting.com
Printed in the USA
BVOW08s2155040117
472672BV00002B/4/P